1000

TIPS AND TOOLS

For

SMALL BUSINESS

SUCCESS

DR. ALI ASADI

To my dear friend Alireza

Ali asadi

er. 8. 20

ISBN: 978-0-578-60974-4
Library of Congress Control Number: 2019918849

Ali Asadi
Asadi Business Consulting, Inc
1403 Lomita Blvd. #107,
Harbor City, CA 90710
www.aasadi.com

This book is dedicated to my loving parents, Mohammad & Ashraf. Without their knowledge, wisdom, and guidance, I would not have the goals I have to strive for and the determination to be the best that I can be to reach my dreams!

Table of Contents

Acknowledgments

Any book cannot be produced without the help and guidance from a number of people. In writing this book, I, too, have received much guidance and help, which I gratefully acknowledge. Here are some people I wish to thank by name.

My parents, Mohammed and Ashraf, have always been an inspiration throughout my life. I truly value their support, guidance, and encouragement.

Dr. Nosrat Nabavi, a dear friend and trusted advisor, whose support has been most welcome during challenging times.

I wish to thank my teachers, who have been such a great inspiration and who taught me to think clearly and logically and prepared me to chart my path. In particular, I want to name Dr. Terry Nolan.

I also want to thank Doug Russell for doing a great job in editing this book.

Thank you all. I look forward to your continued support.

Preface

Why a small business success handbook?

As a business consultant who has been working with various small businesses for more than twenty years, I often find that small-business owners/managers need practical guidance in business management by which they can refer to in different situations. All the thousands of books written by management gurus contain the information business owners/managers seek, but it is seldom organized in a form where one can jump to the information without going through lengthy theory, case studies, surveys, and graphs.

Since I was lacking such an easy-to-use resource for small business management, I decided to get working and produce such a book myself. After all, if I felt this need, surely there are other busy managers who have no time to read big, fat management books in the hope of finding what they need.

This book is a toolkit. If you need an answer to your HR, marketing, and operation management needs, you will find it here. If you want to be more productive, make better decisions, and even find a better business travel deal, you will find tips and tools here, and if you want good books or a smart quote, you will find it here too.

Browse the book as you will, use the table of contents, flip the pages, or just open at a random page. I am sure you will find something you will need—something you did not know before.

I wish you a happy journey of discovery and look forward to feedback and suggestions for additional sections.

Dr. Ali Asadi
www.aasadi.com

Section 1

The Journey of Business Success

There are numerous definitions regarding success and being successful. Here is the definition in *Merriam-Webster's Dictionary*:

"Success is the desired result of an attempt."

This sentence has three main words:

1. Attempt: Success needs commitment and hard work. If it were easy, everyone would be successful. As Vince Lombardi says, *"The only place success comes before work is in the dictionary."*

2. Result: Success is a journey, not an event, but you should have goals to get motivated and have a direction.

3. Desired: Never underestimate yourself! You do not know what you are going to achieve until you try. As Norman Vincent Peale says,

"Shoot for the moon. Even if you miss, you'll land among the stars."

In this regard, there is no need to emphasize that learning new skills is one of the essential ingredients of success in any field.

Jim Rohn says:

"Modify Your Dreams, or Magnify Your Skills!"

And here comes the main question:

Are you Process Oriented or Results Oriented?

Most of us want to achieve our goals and solve our problems as soon as possible; that's why we may ignore the processes that lead to our achievements. This approach is like a hungry person who tries to get full without watching what he is eating. It is obvious that although he gets full, he may end up in a hospital.

A couple of years ago, I had a chance to read the very well-known book *The Power of Now* by Eckhart Tolle. This book has sold millions of copies worldwide and has been translated into more than thirty foreign languages. If you have not read it yet, I highly recommend you do so. One of the main points of this book is that many people are upset about the past and worry about the future that may never come up. Therefore, they never live in the present and enjoy the moment. That's why we even link our success and happiness to other people or a specific destination rather than our present journey.

Please keep in mind that I am not against having goals. Having goals is so important and works as a motivational and inspirational tool in both business and personal life. My point is that success is a journey, not a destination. There is no magical point in life to reach and say, "Wow! I am happy and successful for the rest of my life."

Life is like driving a car; if you just look in the rearview mirror or very far ahead when you drive, you will have an accident for sure. So, you should watch a specific distance ahead and sometimes look in the rearview mirror to learn from your experiences and to consider that your destination has the right direction.

As a business coach, I have seen this issue in many businesses as well. Many people start businesses or add a new product or a service to their lines without preparation. What these people miss is that business success is like taking a road trip. When you are going for a trip, besides knowing your destination, you should check many things, such as the following: Do you have a proper business system (your car engine)? Do you have enough resources (fuel)? Have you checked the traffic (your competitors)? Do you have a good company (your team)? Have you checked the weather (the market) before starting your trip?

In this regard, while you are trying to achieve your professional goals, it is very important to have a balanced life to enjoy your success journey. Let me share a true story with you.

When I first met James in August 2006, he owned a retail store in one of the small cities in Southern California. Although James was a hard worker, he was trying to take care of his health and his family as well. He had recently married and was proud of his choice. As a business coach who had seen many business owners, the emphasis that James put on the balance between work and life was very impressive to me. One day during our meeting, I told him, "James! I enjoy the way you manage your time to take care of your wealth, health, and love life." James took a deep breath and said, "Ali! I learned my lesson in a very hard way." James sipped his ice tea and then started telling me his story.

James used to own a big software company in Northern California. He had an excellent wife and two gorgeous daughters. Whoever looked at his life could say he was the luckiest man in the world. But he was not! James used to work seven days a week from 8:00 a.m. to 9:00 p.m. Most of the time, his daughters fell asleep behind the windows waiting for their dad. And whenever his close friends told him to take care of his family, he always responded, "Let me get my private jet. I will take them on an unforgettable vacation."

Unfortunately, James's calculation did not go well. After the IT market crash in 2001, he ended up with $15 million debt and lost his business. He also lost his family since his wife had already gotten a divorce two months before. To complete the bad luck package, poor James became depressed due to losing all his money and his family.

James told me, "I went from hero to zero! I could not even drive due to high depression." After spending his worst time in life, he started getting therapy and also began his life again with one important point in mind: "Success is the combination of wealth, health, and love." In 2005, James got married again and opened a new retail store. And finally, in 2015, he gained back his wealth while having a lovely family as well. James's story always reminds me of this famous quote, *"Never get too busy making a living that you forget to make a life."*

Now, if you are ready to start your business success journey, let's learn more about the main characteristics of small businesses.

Section 2

Small Businesses Overview

As in almost every country, small businesses have a vital role in the United States economy, which includes 99.9 percent of U.S. businesses and 47.8 percent of nationwide employees. The rate of success among small enterprises, however, is too low, especially in large cities. Based on statistics from the Small Business Administration (SBA), which is a U.S. government agency, one-third of new small companies could survive perhaps only ten years.

Many reasons can be given for the high failure rates of small businesses. Internal causes can be attributed to poor planning and risk management, incorrect decisions, and bad management. External causes of failure include overall difficult economic conditions and a highly competitive environment. Small businesses also sometimes fail to follow regulatory procedures and may not be updated with the latest regulations that control them. Besides, many small-business owners do not have formal managerial training or experience and attempt to run their business intuitively based on their personal experience.

In this regard, some management experts recommend the formalization of business procedures and state that hiring, managing, and retaining capable employees are usually the main challenges of small companies; therefore, having proper human resource management systems may even increase the financial performance of small enterprises. From another perceptive, it has been proven that small businesses that have both short- and long-term plans are more successful in comparison with small enterprises that have no plans. However, a written strategic plan may not necessarily lead to high business performance until it is written carefully by considering different internal and external organizational factors.

As mentioned earlier, many small businesses are adversely affected by not being able to follow or adapt to government rules and regulations covering their area of operations. Due to their limited resources, small businesses can be greatly affected if a new rule comes into force. Further, the performance of small businesses can be greatly influenced by organizational policies and culture, business owners' characteristics, and management procedures. In small companies, organizational culture, which includes common values, norms, and beliefs, is affected by the personality of the business owners, the number of employees, working structure, the technology used, and the types of products or services provided by the businesses.

Now the main question is: what is a small business?

Small Business Definition

There is no globally accepted definition of a small business. Different countries, organizations, and even scholars may choose to define a small business differently. In the U.S., the Office of Advocacy is taken as the representative of the small business community. This office classifies a business as small if it has fewer than five hundred employees. The European Commission, on the other hand, classifies a business as small if it has fewer than two hundred and fifty employees and an annual turnover of less than € 50 million.

To be fair, merely counting the numbers of employees is not the best way to classify businesses. Many technology companies could be generating large profits from a small employee base. In such a case, income criteria seem to be better suited to define a small business. There can even be a mixed approach to this classification. Such a method may use both quantitative and qualitative criteria to classify a business. Qualitatively, we could go by the ownership and hierarchy pattern of the business, whereas quantitatively, we could use such things as employee count and turnover to classify the business.

Small Business Characteristics

Whatever classification criterion one may employ, certain key characteristics are common to most small businesses, as the following:

- The organizational structure is flatter, allowing better communication between employees.
- Management is small and flexible, leading to faster decisions.
- Resources are limited.
- There is generally a lack of clear boundaries in employee tasks and positions.
- Decision-making is often an individual responsibility and not a collective process.
- Multitasking is the norm. Both owners and employees may wear many hats and perform different duties at different times.

In this regard, the need for multitasking in small companies may lead to friction and conflict. This is particularly so in small, family-run businesses. In such businesses, success is often dependent on the flexibility to accept market and organizational changes, leveraging new technology, agility, and rapid decision-making and gaining a first-mover advantage. In such a fluid environment, the personality and tenacity of the small-business owner become important determinants of success.

Successful small-business owners understand that no small business can be a scaled-down version of a large corporation. There are fundamental differences between the two. Small businesses score on flat governance structure, rapid communication, and decision-making. However, they suffer from a lack of resources, capital, and managerial expertise. Since many small-business owners lack managerial knowledge, their management style tends to be intuitive and hands-on. As a consequence, they may lack legal and financial knowledge, which can be a major impediment as the business grows.

Many small businesses start off informally without a well-structured business plan. The owner/manager works things out mentally and does not need to draw a plan or keep detailed records. Some owners may downplay the importance of a business plan and detailed records. As the business grows, however, the shortcomings of such a method become evident. There is a clear generational gap in the way small-business owners approach planning and documentation. The older generation of small-business owners tends to be more hands-on in running operations and may run the business intuitively without much time for business plans and documentation. Younger entrepreneurs have grown with technology and have no hesitation in using modern techniques and structured processes to run their business.

The limited ability to handle risk is another characteristic of small businesses. Resources and managerial expertise are limited, and hence the small business is restricted in its ability to absorb shocks. Being excessively conservative in handling resources may provide a risk cushion but will impede the growth of the business. A balancing game needs to be played, and very often, it is the attitude of the manager/owner that will define the capability of the business to handle unforeseen risks.

Small Business Success Factors

Many internal and external factors affect small business success, including decisions by business owners, competition, organizational culture and structure, knowledge and training, and industry structure. If we consider small business growth as an index of success, resources, and organizational procedures to use resources have a direct effect on organizational growth. From another view, while most small-business owners rely on prior knowledge and experience, new knowledge and training have a significant impact on small business success.

We all know that due to globalization and increased competition, small businesses have faced many operational challenges; therefore, they must invest in new ways of gaining market share, collaborating with other players, learning and applying knowledge, and adapting information technology. Innovation in small businesses must be comprehensive and not only should it be in products or services but also in hiring and managing employees, marketing, and other business procedures. Unfortunately, in most small companies, employees are not encouraged or rewarded to share their ideas; therefore, innovative ideas may only be generated by business owners. Many small businesses are run by people who are too dominating and may not be willing to accept new ideas from employees. With such owners/managers, it is their way or the highway.

Similarly, a small business may have a situation where early hires or family members have a disproportionate influence on decision-making. This proximity to power can often become a barrier in the generation of new ideas. In case such a barrier develops in a small business, then it takes away a key advantage a small business has over a large one.

One way to break these barriers is to develop an organizational culture in which all employees are encouraged to not only express their opinions but also to share the new knowledge with each other. This continuous churn of new ideas will keep the business fresh and

9

ensure that management does not become too complacent. Luckily, bringing about change in the organizational culture of a small company is far easier than in a large enterprise. The key issue to understand is the importance of good leadership in a small business. Leadership sets the direction and strategy of the business.

Leadership in Small Businesses

Management of a business is concerned with routine operations, while leadership defines the vision and values. Effective leaders lay down the ground rules for how managers and employees must conduct themselves as they run the business. In a small business, where there are only a few people, the personality of a leader can make an enormous difference. The leader influences how the team interacts with customers and partners and how it performs and reacts in good and bad times. There are two sides to a leader's personality—a professional side and a personal dimension. Both are critically important.

On the professional front, a great leader demonstrates the following:

- A constant push for improvement and a transition from a good business to a great business.

- Clearly shows a focus on long-term benefits regardless of the difficulties involved.

- Sets the standards for professional behavior.

- Takes responsibility rather than apportioning blame.

Personally, a leader shows humility and prevents the development of a culture where he/she is taken to be a perfect figure that can do no wrong. Therefore, on the personal front, a good small-business leader shows the following characteristics:

- Modesty — the leader does not boast or take credit for things that go well with the business. This person is generous and credits team members for the good work (while accepting any blame for the mistakes).

- Quiet calm and determination — A good leader brings a sense of calm to the business. The leader ensures that employees can work in peace and are not scared of taking the initiative that may sometimes not yield the desired result.

- Ambition not for self but for the business — The leader is ambitious but not for personal gain. This person understands that the business is bigger than any individual, and he or she will show this in his or her daily work ethic.

- Sets up successors — Many business managers tend to believe that the company will collapse if they leave. A good leader knows that they are not the ultimate fountain of knowledge and will groom a successor well in time.

Good leadership leads to good decision-making processes in the business. Once again, since the resources are limited and the business is small, the impact of each decision will be large.

Decision-Making in Small Businesses

In a large business, any decision usually goes through a well-structured process, with experts examining the technical, financial, and marketing aspects of the decision in detail. If any of these domains points out a shortcoming, a correction is called for and is usually applied before proceeding further. This process of "due diligence" minimizes bad decisions. The process can be very different in a small business. Most decision-makers in a small business would be the owners themselves. Their previous experiences may create biases that affect future decisions. For example, a business owner not very familiar with online sales and purchases may choose to neglect the opportunities offered by the Internet and thereby deprive the business of new areas of growth and efficiency.

There is sometimes a tendency to simplify the decision-making process, basing it on superficial or surface inputs and not looking

11

deep enough for second order effects of the decision. This happens when an entrepreneur takes decisions based on his/her personal knowledge alone rather than using a 360-degree approach that combines input from others as well. Owners also seem to feel that running a small business requires them to make instantaneous decisions. There is also a sense of (false) pride in appearing to be very decisive.

The limited resilience of a small business amplifies the impact of each decision. Therefore, there is a reason to be deliberate and careful in making business decisions. It is important to set up checklists and processes to ensure that all dimensions of a decision are carefully examined before committing the business to a course of action.

Risk Management in Small Enterprises

The other area that both affects and is affected by the mindset of small business owners is risk management. In cases where small businesses use less complicated business processes, enterprises might be more flexible to various changes but might be more risk vulnerable due to a lack of enough resources. Although small companies are high-risk ventures, most of them do not have the knowledge and even formal risk management systems to study internal weaknesses and external threats.

From a different perspective, small businesses can handle potential risks better than large corporations due to the fast decision-making process, multitasking employees who can help each other, and easy informal communications between employers and employees. As mentioned before, there is no general recommendation for different small companies. In my opinion, fast decision-making may not always be helpful in risk management since it may ignore researching new information and potential threats in any organization. I have seen in many cases that oversimplification and a lack of formal procedures lead to missing important issues and consequently undesirable results. Successful small-business owners not only supplement their entrepreneurship skills with managerial knowledge but also they are more proactive than reactive regarding external changes. In this regard, in small companies, due to a lack of enough resources and expertise, developing a risk management strategy is not an easy task. One of the main steps is to learn about small-business owners' perceptions of risk by defining different scenarios of things that might happen and analyzing their responses. Small-business owners' characteristics and even gender and age have a direct effect on their approaches and strategies in dealing with business risks.

Change Management in Small Companies

Small companies are more receptive to external changes due to their flexibility and informal business procedures and channels of communication. While in large corporations, change is a delayed process, in small companies, an effective change is a rapid response to external changes, which may bring competitive advantages. In small companies, change management is closely connected to the characteristics of business owners. From another view, since most small business owners are the main change initiators, their attitude and personal objectives have a direct effect on organizational changes.

In general, various factors that develop a successful change in a small company are 1) flexibility of business procedures and management systems, 2) support of stakeholders, 3) cooperation and collaboration among organizational members, and 4) continuation of learning and skill development.

Learning and Knowledge Creation in Small Enterprises

New knowledge and innovations are the main elements of success in a competitive business environment; however, the prerequisites of learning and welcoming outside knowledge are the quality and quantity of the current knowledge and learning mechanism in small companies. In small companies, knowledge sharing happens through cross-functionality and overlapping roles; however, business owners are creators and facilitators of the knowledge management process. In this regard, two main factors that affect learning in small companies are 1) learning the behavior of organizational members, which includes personal characteristics and learning styles, and 2) the learning environment, which is affected by organizational culture, structure, and procedures. Learning in small companies is mostly just in time, informal, and by trial and error.

What differentiates small companies from large enterprises are different managerial practices and limited resources, which may constrain learning and knowledge management in small companies; however, having a flexible organizational structure and informal communication may expedite the learning process in small companies. In this regard, learning through practice, which mainly is based on responding to internal and external uncertainties, is one of the main characteristics of knowledge creation in small companies.

As mentioned earlier, since small-business owners are the primary decision-makers and have a crucial role in knowledge development and implementation, knowledge is more subjective, experiential, and informal. In this regard, small-business owners usually face problems in implementing formal training and general information, which are not customizable and applicable to their specific business needs.

Accordingly, the openness of small-business owners to new knowledge is one of the primary elements in organizational learning and knowledge management in small companies. However, even if a small-business owner is open to new knowledge, many factors impede transferring the knowledge internally, such as the inability to identify the required knowledge, generational and cultural gaps, and lack of enough motivation and incentives among organizational members. That is one of the areas that business consultants can help small businesses dramatically by analyzing business procedures, identifying deficiencies, and transferring the new knowledge to improve them.

So far, we have reviewed the main characteristics of small businesses and the factors that make a successful business. Now, let's learn tips and tools in various topics. Please keep in mind that knowledge is not power; implementing knowledge is power. So, try to implement whatever you learn in this book. If you have any questions, please contact me through my website https://www.aasadi.com/

Section 3

Business Success Tips & Tools

This section includes thousands of tips, tools, and other resources in various management and professional topics. If you need an answer to your HR, marketing, and operation management needs, you will find it here. If you want to be more productive, make better decisions, and even find a better business travel deal, you will find tips and tools here, and if you want good books or a smart quote, you will find it here too.

Browse this section as you will, use the table of contents, flip the pages, or just open at a random page. I am sure you will find something you will need — something you did not know before.

Management & Self Improvement

How to Start a Business if You Do not Have a Business Idea

Why is it Important?

Knowing how to start a business prepares you for much more than simply running your business. At the most basic level, it teaches you the rules and regulations and how a small business is structured. Even more importantly, though, it teaches you to take ownership of your actions, to interact with people, to observe the market and market conditions, and to think about starting something that can eventually be bigger than anything you may have done before.

Learning about how to start a business also gives you confidence that you are no longer tied down to a job that is controlled by someone else. You are in charge of and responsible for your destiny. You will be the one who will generate employment and be responsible for the growth of your company. A person starting a business for the first time shows that he has confidence in his capability and the courage to venture into unfamiliar territory. This does not mean that you jump in unprepared. You must study the market, know your strengths, and build a strong team. Knowing how to start a business makes good business sense!

Quotes from Successful People

- *"Make something people want includes making a company that people want to work for."* — **Sahil Lavingia**

- *"Even if you don't have the perfect idea to begin with, you can likely adapt."* — **Victoria Ransom**

- *"Chase the vision, not the money; the money will end up following you."* — **Tony Hsieh**

- *"Don't worry about failure; you only have to be right once."* — **Drew Houston**

- *"Any time is a good time to start a company."* — **Ron Conway**

10 Great Tips

1. Take a piece of paper and write down your goals, strengths, and weaknesses in both your personal and professional life.

2. Keep in mind that to have a successful business, you must love what you do, be very good at it, and find markets for your products or services.

3. Search to determine what frustrates people so that your product or service could solve the issue.

4. Sometimes you do not need to create a new product or service; see if you can make current products and services better or less expensive.

5. Review different options and test your ideas by developing samples and getting feedback from potential customers.

6. Keep in mind that if you can use your own product or service, other people may find it helpful as well.

7. Educate yourself about current regulations and technological trends in the industry you are going to work in.

8. Review current players in the market, including competitors, collaborators, and customers.

9. Write an effective business plan, but be flexible to revise it later.

10. Consult with a business mentor.

Tools and Resources

1. Book: *The Lean Startup: How Today's Entrepreneurs Use Continuous Innovation to Create Radically Successful Businesses*, by Eric Ries https://amzn.to/2ZqUol5

2. Book: *The Startup Checklist: 25 Steps to a Scalable, High-Growth Business*, by David S. Rose https://amzn.to/2HoxOTR

3. Book: *The $100 Startup: Reinvent the Way You Make a Living, Do What You Love, and Create a New Future*, by Chris Guillebeau https://amzn.to/2NxeRCn

4. Book: *Small Business Start-Up Kit, The: A Step-by-Step Legal Guide*, by Peri Pakroo J.D. https://amzn.to/2UezZPr

5. TaskQue - https://taskque.com/ - A cloud-based task management tool that is ideal for entrepreneurs. Manage your projects and keep track of those bright ideas.

How to Franchise Your Business

Why is it Important?

There are several ways to grow your business. One way is to grow it organically one outlet at a time with you putting in all the hard work. This takes time and patience and, of course, capital. The other way is to first build your business into something that most people recognize and value and then to franchise it into a number of outlets—run by different people, all following your business philosophy and standards—and paying you money for the privilege.

If you have been able to build a strong presence in the market and have a product that is sought after by a large number of people in different parts of the country, then franchising the business is a great option. This may not be an easy path, but if you do succeed, the benefits amount to continuous cash flow and business expansion without much additional work.

Franchising means a lot of legal work and a very rigid and standardized workflow. However, once the process is set up, growth is simply a repetition of something that has already been proven to work.

Quotes from Successful People

- *"Our greatest weakness lies in giving up. The most certain way to succeed is always to try just one more time."* — **Thomas Edison**

- *"A creative man is motivated by the desire to achieve, not by the desire to beat others."* — **Ayn Rand**

- *"Without hard work, nothing grows but weeds."* — **Gordon Hinckley**

- *"Aim for the moon. If you miss, you may hit a star."* — **W. Clement Stone**

- *"At the end of the day, you just want to go to a team that believes in you . . . and hopefully wants to build a franchise around you."* — **Carson Wentz**

10 Great Tips

1. Develop a successful brand. Your brand represents the value you propose, your organization's culture, beliefs, and the way you take care of your customers.

2. Conduct complete market research to see if there is a good demand for your products or services in various locations.

3. Build an effective system for your business. Having a system means best management practices to run your business in different areas, such as sales, marketing, human resource management, and operations.

4. Create a complete operational manual for different divisions of your business. This can be used for training and reviewing working procedures.

5. It is recommended to have at least three locations before trying to franchise your business. Having more locations shows that your business is replicable, which will make it more attractive to your potential franchisees.

6. Learn about the costs and benefits of franchising your business. That may include legal fees, registration, marketing materials, and business system development training.

7. Get legal advice and learn all laws and regulations regarding franchising in your industry.

8. Have a great team. Franchising your business is totally separate from your day-to-day business activities, so you need to have a great team to manage this new part of your business.

9. Create a solid screening procedure to accept franchisees. That may include personal characteristics, financial backgrounds, and ethical values.

10. Finalize your franchise model, including franchise fee, agreement, marketing, training program you offer, and how you support franchisees.

Tools and Resources

1. IFA - https://www.franchise.org/ - The International Franchise Association is the place to start when you begin to think about franchising your business. You will find invaluable tools, literature, and ideas on this website.

2. Franchise Expo - https://www.ifeinfo.com/ - The International Franchise Expo gives you opportunities to meet other entrepreneurs and business owners. Network with like-minded people and grow.

3. Franchise publications - https://www.franchising.com/ - Contact possible business partners across countries over many different types of media, get access to professional magazines, and track franchisee conferences, all from a single website.

4. Proven Match - https://provenmatch.com/ - Analyze your franchise operations with a solution specifically tailored to franchisee operations. Proven Match also helps you in franchisee selection so that you do not end up with expensive mistakes.

5. Franchise Documents -http://www.freefranchisedocs.com/
   - A lot of legal work and documentation is involved in setting up a franchise. Get free templates of the documents on this website.

How to Get a Franchised Business

Why is it Important?

Many entrepreneurs have found that a good way to get a foothold in business is to pick a strategy and a business model that has already been proven to work. The costs to set up a franchised venture are usually very well defined. You know exactly what you are getting into and have opportunities to see the chain in action. The parent company will generally look after the brand building and the advertising and will provide the required training and technical documentation. Raising funds for getting into a franchise agreement is often much easier compared with starting a fresh business because banks understand the business model and may have financed other franchises of the same business as well.

In most cases, the franchisee will be able to select the city or locality he will work in. Being familiar with the local conditions will help the new businessman generate leads faster and build better connections with clients. Eventually, you may be able to expand your franchise to include more outlets.

Quotes from Successful People

- *"Ability is what you're capable of doing. Motivation determines what you do. Attitude determines how well you do it."* — **Lou Holtz**

- *"The insurance of working with a big, already successful franchise just gives you the chance to do other things on a more personal level."* — **Jason Statham**

- *"The franchise itself gives no real power, unless accompanied by the right on the part of all the possessors of it to elect something like an equal number of representatives."* — **John Bright**

- *"For a franchise system to work well, you really need people with an entrepreneurial mind-set because, while you have a large, overarching system that everybody has to work with, a lot of local issues have to be handled."* — **Fred DeLuca**

- *"Again, a franchise to me doesn't have to be a billion-dollar title."* — **David Fincher**

10 Great Tips

1. Be clear about your objectives of purchasing a franchise business.

2. Do you have enough time and financial resources to get involved in a franchise?

3. Learn about the pros and cons of purchasing a franchise business.

4. Learning about the 5Cs (Company, Customer, Competitor, Collaborators, and Climate of the market) can give you a complete view of the franchise.

5. Learn about all expenses of having a franchise business, such as entry fees, royalties, and operational expenses.

6. Conduct a lot of research and review your options. There are many online resources that can help you find a good franchise.

7. Try to collect as much as information you can, such as financial statements and newspaper articles. Ask for Uniform Franchise Offering Circulars (UFOCs).

8. If you have difficulties in interpreting numbers, hire an accountant to understand all numbers clearly.

9. Interview the franchisor and a couple of the current and former franchisees to get a better view of the business.

10. Get legal advice and learn all laws and regulations regarding franchising in your industry.

Tools and Resources

1. Score - https://www.score.org/franchising-resources - Start off on the right foot. Check out a long list of "must-know" franchisee information.

2. Franchise Guides - https://www.franchising.com - Learn about franchising opportunities in many different domains. Some cost less than $5,000 to start!

3. Franchising Direct - https://www.franchisedirect.com/ - Find hundreds of franchising opportunities in practically any country you can name. Search by industry, location, or investment amount.

4. Search a Franchise - https://www.franchisegator.com/ - Get your franchise business going in a flash. Use the Franchisegator search tool to find a franchise that suits you.

5. Franchise Opportunities- https://www.franchiseopportunities.com/ - Find large numbers of franchising opportunities and get some very helpful tips on how to handle your franchise search.

How to Hire a Business Lawyer

Why is it Important?

Many small-business owners think they can delay hiring a business lawyer until their business gets bigger, or they actually run into a legal issue or get sued. This is absolutely the wrong way to approach the issue. The right time to engage a business lawyer is when you start the business so that proper guidance can be given and early mistakes avoided. Hiring a lawyer early on in the life of the business is a good idea because the lawyer can grow with your business and guide you about copyrights and patents and about registering any trademarks.

This can save you enormous trouble later on. We have seen many businesses face big troubles that were avoidable and happened due to the lack of knowledge regarding legal matters.

Many experienced business lawyers can also give you good advice about how to manage the administrative aspects of your business. You need to be aware of the legal issues involved in managing your employees. There are important rules and regulations to be aware of if you have to fire an employee or conduct a background check. Getting advice on such matters early on can help you stay focused on the core business rather than on frustrating problems.

Quotes from Successful People

- *"The power of the lawyer is in the uncertainty of the law."* — **Jeremy Bentham**

- *"Being a lawyer is not merely a vocation. It is a public trust, and each of us has an obligation to give back to our communities."* — **Janet Reno**

- *"Discipline is part of my professional training as a lawyer."* — **Mohamed ElBaradei**

- *"In seeking a lawyer, you are looking for an advocate, an expert advisor on the law and on your rights and responsibilities, a strategist, a negotiator, and a litigator."* — **Laura Wasser**

- *"The main business of a lawyer is to take the romance, the mystery, the irony, the ambiguity out of everything he touches."* — **Antonin Scalia**

10 Great Tips

1. Know exactly what specialty you are looking for, such as a tax attorney, transactional lawyer, or an intellectual property attorney.

2. Ask people you trust to refer good lawyers with that specialty.

3. Search to get an idea about attorneys' fees and compensation of similar cases.

4. Get a free consultation session if possible.

5. See if the lawyer has worked with similar cases. Is he familiar with your industry?

6. See if the lawyer is interested in your business, and you can get along with each other.

7. See how responsive your attorney is with you. Lawyers who are too busy to respond to their clients will not be effective although they might be famous.

8. Lawyers may have different billing strategies, such as hourly, flat fee, retainer, and contingent fee. Do not forget to discuss the billing strategy that fits your situation the best.

9. If the project is very specific without unknown factors, it is much better to go per case than an hourly fee so that you know in advance how much you are going to spend.

10. Be prepared before meeting your lawyer. Have all the required documents ready and also search through reliable sources to be familiar with your needs.

Tools and Resources

1. Law Guru - https://www.lawguru.com/ - Get free answers to your legal questions answered by qualified attorneys.

2. Lawers.com- https://www.lawyers.com/legal-info/business-law/ - A whole list of commonly asked questions you can refer to.

3. Legal Shield - https://www.legalshield.com/ - Find suitable lawyers near you and get low-cost monthly legal assistance from real lawyers. Emergency help is also available.

4. Legal Zoom - https://www.legalzoom.com - Low-cost prepaid attorney assistance plans.

5. FindLaw - https://smallbusiness.findlaw.com/ - Specifically tailored to small businesses, this site will help you with

opening a business to finally closing it and everything else you may encounter in between.

How to Know if You Need a Business Consultant

Why is it Important?

A small-business owner has to wear many hats. This can sometimes cause problems because many owners do not have expertise in every possible field of the business. Sometimes it is required to get an alternative view of the issues affecting the business. The problems that may be troubling the business and preventing it from growing may not even be understood correctly. This is where a consultant can come in.

Companies have to deal with thousands of problems as they grow. Solving these problems can take an effort that may take the focus away from the core activity of the company. An experienced business consultant can solve these problems for you more efficiently than you could yourself. The consultant will bring in the specialist knowledge of the subject and has experience and contacts in the field that can help the business in its early years. In many cases, we have seen small companies grow very rapidly and miss out on certain fundamental practices. For example, if you are outsourcing a part of your manufacturing, the consultant could help ensure that your contract is comprehensive and well-drawn. This would ensure that your outsourcing processes are correct and your interests are fully protected. Left to yourself, you could make mistakes that would hurt your business.

Quotes from Successful People

- *"My greatest strength as a consultant is to be ignorant and ask a few questions."* — **Peter Drucker**

- *"As technology makes it easier for a business to find and collaborate with outside expertise, a huge and competitive market for consultants will arise."* — **Bill Gates**

- *"In the business world, everyone is paid in two coins: cash and experience. Take the experience first; the cash will come later."* — **Harold Geneen**

- *"The price of anything is the amount of life you exchange for it."* — **Henry David Thoreau**

- *"I feel that luck is preparation meeting opportunity."* — **Oprah Winfrey**

10 Great Tips

1. One idea may change your business forever. You should hire a business consultant in different situations, especially the following:

2. When you need to invest more in your business.

3. When you need to write a great business plan.

4. When you need to check on your business performance.

5. When you want to start a new business.

6. When you need to hire effective employees.

7. When you have problems with your current staff.

8. When you want to get more customers.

9. When you want to save a lot of time and money.

10. When you want to learn new management skills.

Tools and Resources

1. Book: *Business Adventures*, by John Brooks
   https://amzn.to/2ZtRJHo

2. Book: *How to Win Friends & Influence People*, by Dale Carnegie https://amzn.to/2ZoI7Od

3. Book: *Think and Grow Rich!*, by Napoleon Hill
   https://amzn.to/328SQOz

4. Book: *The 7 Habits of Highly Effective People*, by Stephen R. Covey https://amzn.to/327kueu

5. Book: *Good to Great: Why Some Companies Make the Leap and Others Don't*, by Jim Collins https://amzn.to/2U37F2j

How to Get Helped by a Business Coach

Why is it Important?

We live in a world where change is the only constant; businesses keep evolving and become more competitive. In such a scenario, it is difficult to keep up with changes in the industry and the marketplace as well as learning new business success tools and techniques. Accordingly, having a business coach isn't a luxury but rather a necessity for steering your business to safety and prosperity.

Like a human body, every business or organization has different parts and sections, such as marketing, human resources, accounting, or inventory, which could represent human organs. A management and decision-making section would be the brain, and employees would be like cells in our body.

Now, as you evaluate your body and mind to determine if you have any problems or need to visit a physician or a therapist, it is highly recommended also to evaluate the business you own or manage to make sure everything is working properly or if you need to solve any issues before they become critical. That's where business coaches and consultants come to the page.

A business coach can give you a true picture of your business and suggest new ideas to improve it. Whether you are well established or just starting off, you will always benefit from the advice of a good business coach, who will show you different tools and techniques that will help your business succeed. If you are going to hire new employees, market your products or services, cut your business expenses, or manage other business practices, a business coach can help you understand the issues involved and make the right decisions.

Quotes from Successful People

- *"A coach is someone who tells you what you don't want to hear, who has you see what you don't want to see, so you can be who you always knew you could be."* — **Tom Landry**

- *"All coaching is, is taking a player where he can't take himself."* — **Bill McCartney**

- *"Probably my best quality as a coach is that I ask a lot of challenging questions and let the person come up with the answer."* — **Phil Dixon**

- *"The goal of coaching is the goal of good management: to make the most of an organization's valuable resources."* — **Harvard Business Review**

- *"Coaches have to watch for what they don't want to see and listen to what they don't want to hear."* — **John Madden**

10 Great Tips

1. In today's changing and competitive business environment, it is difficult to keep up with changes in the industry and the marketplace as well as learning new business success tools and techniques. Therefore, getting a business coach isn't a luxury but a necessity that you must have to steer your business to safety and prosperity.

2. Hiring a business coach is an investment that can bring your business many short- and long-term benefits.

3. A business coach can help you write your business plan to get business loans, find investors, start your business, and analyze your current business situation.

4. A business coach can help you manage your business like your body or your car to find the issues and solve them before they become critical.

5. A business coach gives you a true picture of your business and brings new ideas to improve it. Whether you are well established or just starting off, you will always gain from the advice of a good business coach.

6. A coach will show you different tools and techniques that will help your business succeed. If you are going do such things as, hire new employees, market your products or services, or cut your business expenses, a business coach can help you understand the issues involved and help you make the right decisions.

7. Business coaching aids you in becoming more open and receptive to various innovative techniques of marketing your products and services. Business improvement techniques, such as process classification, planning, automation, and improvement, can be difficult to handle if your firm has never done them before.

8. A business coach saves you a lot of time and money by providing the best management practices and helping you in implementing them.

9. A business coach can help you make better decisions by looking at the issues from other aspects that you may overlook.

10. A business coach can teach you great business management skills, such as time management, negotiation, employee management, cost management, communication, and much more.

Tools and Resources

1. Score - https://www.score.org/ - Find a mentor who will help you run your business efficiently and succeed in the marketplace. Score from the Small Business Administration is built to help entrepreneurs.

2. Expert Help - http://www.aasadi.com/ - Consult with Dr. Ali Asadi and get your business on the fast track. Proven methods help you avoid mistakes that can drag you down.

3. Micro Mentor - https://www.micromentor.org - Micro Mentor is a nonprofit network that connects entrepreneurs with volunteer consultants who can help your business prosper.

4. Vistage - https://www.vistage.com - An organization with branches in various locations to help professionals in different industries.

5. Association of Women's Business Centers - https://www.awbc.org/ - A great organization to help businesswomen be more successful.

How to Choose Your Business Location

Why is it Important?

Choosing the correct location for your business can be the difference between success and failure. It is not enough to get cheap land or buildings. You need to check raw material, availability of qualified workforce, markets, and transportation. Different states may have different laws, and these could also have a major effect on your business.

Even if you are running a small business, you may be using components made in different states or even countries. Under such circumstances, it might be beneficial to be located near a transport hub. Many businesses locate themselves near sources of raw materials to reduce costs and get reliable access to supplies.

Being in a cluster also helps. You may have noticed that many automobile component manufacturers are located close to each other in a cluster. Clustering helps in getting trained human resources with ease and being able to discuss and solve similar types of problems together. One great example is the Silicon Valley, where large numbers of entrepreneurs, software programmers, and venture capitalists get together to create synergy.

Once you have made investments in buildings and other facilities, it can get very expensive to shift your business location. Therefore, it is very important to take your time and select a good location right in the beginning.

Quotes from Successful People

- *"Making money is art and working is art and good business is the best art."* — **Andy Warhol**

- *"Something like 80 per cent of business decisions have a location element. In fact, it's probably higher than that."* — **Jack Dangermond**

- *"The precept that location is key to the success of a business applies to art, and even to life itself: we thrive or wither depending on how nourishing our environment is."* — **Yann Martel**

- *"Wrong location? Move it. Wrong people? Replace 'em. Wrong industry? I don't believe it. I've got a company in the machine tools industry, and we're doing great. I'd happily go into the coal business. It's how you look at something and how it's managed that make the difference."* — **Ken Hendricks**

- *"The three most important things in retail are location, location, location. The three most important things for our consumer business are technology, technology, technology."* — **Jeff Bezos**

10 Great Tips

1. First, you need to know how important your location is for your customers. Is your location easily accessible to them?

2. Keep in mind that your business location must be consistent with your brand. Check out the demographic of the neighborhood.

3. What is the history of the location and former businesses that used to operate in this location?

4. How close is your location to your suppliers?

5. How close is the location to your competitors?

6. What legal matters do you need to consider for your business location? Make sure there is no legal or zoning restriction to conduct business in this location.

7. What are the future developing plans in your neighborhood?

8. Make sure that you have already checked the building, required repairs, and other expenses, such as utility costs.

9. If you have walk-in customers, are there enough parking spaces available for them?

10. As the business owner, how convenient is your location for you? It is recommended that your business location be close to where you live so that you can manage it more effectively and efficiently.

Tools and Resources

1. Targomo - https://www.targomo.com/ - Want to find a great location for your business based on parameters you specify? Targomo gives you everything you need.

2. Mapcite - https://www.mapcite.com/ - Visualize your business location, target population, supply routes, and practically anything else on the map. No need to learn GIS concepts. Just load your data and requirements and go!

3. Clever analytics - https://www.cleveranalytics.com/ - Are you looking for the best area to start your business? This is a great tool to do market analysis before starting your business.

4. Esri - https://www.esri.com - An effective mapping and analysis software that works in different industries.

5. Census Business Builder (CBB) - https://cbb.census.gov - One of the best places to help you find the best location for your business.

How to Write a Business Plan

Why is it Important?

Do you know how a building is built? What do you think the first step would be? As I am sure you must have guessed, it's the design of the building or the blueprint.

A business plan is also like the blueprint of a building. A well-made business plan gives a panoramic view of the business you want to build. A plan gives a clear picture of what your business will look like. Much like our blueprint, you can now point at things you like or don't like and make necessary changes. Instead of a hazy idea, such as "I want to manufacture faucets," now you have a plan answering such questions as "Where will I get the material?", "How much money do I need?", "Where will I store my product?" and "What is my potential market?"

Now that you know the importance of a business plan, it is clear that it needs to be a good one. An effective business plan, first of all, needs to be well researched. No amount of research is enough. It needs to address all the issues, yet it must be clear and easy to follow. You must use graphs judiciously because it is the best way to present and analyze data. Moreover, you must not overburden the reader with data, so it must be presented in a simple and logical manner.

Quotes from Successful People

- *"Plan for what is difficult while it is easy, do what is great while it is small."* — **Sun Tzu**

- *"By failing to prepare, you are preparing to fail."* — **Benjamin Franklin**

- *"If you don't know where you are going, you'll end up someplace else."* — **Yogi Berra**

- *"A goal without a plan is just a wish."* — **Antoine de Saint-Exupery**

- *"To accomplish great things, we must not only act but also dream. Not only plan but also believe."* — **Anatole France**

10 Great Tips

1. Learn about the outline of a business plan. Search reliable sources to find templates and samples.

2. Write a mission statement and indicate your business objectives.

3. Conduct a 5Cs analysis. This stands for company, customer, competitor, collaborators, and climate of the market.

4. Develop a complete marketing plan, including how you are going to get and keep your customers.

5. Have a complete financial analysis, including projected profit and loss, balance sheet, and cash flow statement for the next three to five years.

6. Develop the list of your current employees and what new positions need to be filled to have a successful operation.

7. Create an action plan to achieve your business goals.

8. If you want to get a loan or need an investment, please indicate how much you need and how you are going to pay them off.

9. Ask a business consultant to review your business plan.

10. Review your plan once in a while and be flexible to make changes if needed.

Tools and Resources

1. Free Plans - https://www.bplans.com/ - Start with these 500 free templates. You are sure to find one that fits your needs. Customize as necessary.

2. Enloop - https://enloop.com/ - A supremely easy-to-use online tool that can create a business plan quickly. It simply provides the data it asks for and gets a finished business plan that you can customize further. This tool supports more than 100 different currency symbols.

3. Score - https://www.score.org/ - If the financial aspects of business plans prove daunting, Score has a list of templates that will help you plan better.

4. Liveplan - https://www.liveplan.com - One of the best business plan developing software with many templates.

5. Small Business Administration - https://www.sba.gov/ - A great website with step-by-step guidance to write your business plan.

How to Choose a Great Business Name

Why is it Important?

Have you heard of a company called Lucky-GoldStar? If you haven't, then you might be surprised to know that it is the earlier name of LG Corporation.

In 1995, to compete in the Western market, Lucky-GoldStar changed its name to LG., and apparently it worked! Today, LG ranks high in the U.S. home appliances market. Although their success cannot be attributed to their change in name alone, it is reasonable to say that it was important.

With many companies selling their goods globally, names have become more important than ever before. Very often, a name that strikes a positive chord in the home country of a company can have a derogatory meaning in another language. Smart businesses spend a lot of effort to make sure their names cannot be misconstrued in other markets.

So when you decide to name your company, you must get information about how it sounds to your potential customers. Ultimately, what matters is not how the name sounds to you but how it sounds to your customers.

Quotes from Successful People

- *"Your reputation is more important than your paycheck, and your integrity is worth more than your career."* — **Ryan Freitas**

- *"Get five or six of your smartest friends in a room and ask them to rate your idea."* — **Mark Pincus**

- *"Get big quietly, so you don't tip off potential competitors."* — **Chris Dixon**

- *"Don't play games that you don't understand, even if you see lots of other people making money from them."* — **Tony Hsieh**

- *"There's no shortage of remarkable ideas, what's missing is the will to execute them."* — **Seth Godin**

10 Great Tips

1. Your business name should be unique and memorable.

2. Choose a name that can be easily spelled by people. Don't use confusing words, such as "for," "4," or "four."

3. Don't choose a name that has no meaning to people unless you invented something that can be a successful brand, such as Google or Yahoo.

4. Make it short and simple. It is recommended to choose a business name with two syllables. Avoid hyphens and special characters.

5. Choose a name that matches with products or services you are going to sell.

6. Think about the future. As an example, it is better not to add geographical names to your business name unless you have no plans to expand your business to other locations.

7. Check to see if the name is available. You can check different government websites or offices to see if the name is available.

8. Try to have the same name for your business and a domain name for your website. This way people can find you much easier on the Internet and your marketing activities will be more effective.

9. Do not choose a name that is similar to that of large companies or your competitors since it can be confusing for your customers.

10. Before registering your business, test the name and ask your potential customers their opinions about your business name.

Tools and Resources

1. Anadea - https://anadea.info/tools/online-business-name-generator - Choosing an awesome business name gets easier than ever before. This great web tool helps you with a name for your company, business, or App.

2. Wordlab - https://www.wordlab.com/ - A crowdsourced resource that gives you more than 7 million options to name your business. You also get help on slogans and taglines.

3. Business Name Generator - https://businessnamegenerator.com/ - Put in some keywords in the search box and get a list of possible names you can select from. This website offers immediate help with domain names and also checks if the domain names are available.

4. Dot-o-mator - https://www.dotomator.com/ - Select some words from a drop-down list or type your own, combine them using Dot-o-mator, and you get several options to name

your business. Dot-o-mator also works for websites and iPhone apps.

5. Name Smith - https://namesmith.io/ - Generate names for your business and domain names for your website all at once. Use up to five keywords and select from scores of choices.

How to Develop a Business Partnership

Why is it Important?

If you think about it, many of the great companies are born out of a partnership. You may have heard of Hewlett and Packard, Jobs and Wozniak, Gates and Allen, and, of course, bane to the empire Solo and Chewbacca (of *Star Wars* fame, in case you are unaware).

A partnership in itself is no guarantee for success, but a great partnership might just be. It is hard for one person to handle all the issues that come with starting a business. A partner who shares a common goal and the same work ethic will help reduce the workload on one person.

Very often, in a successful partnership, each partner brings different skills to the table and helps round out the individual limitations. A partnership may bring a set of checks and balances as well. It is difficult to make mistakes if you have another person double-checking your work and decisions. It has been seen that a business owner gets carried away and makes investment decisions without thinking deeply enough. At such times, having a partner who can cross-check facts and offer an alternate point of view can be a big help.

Quotes from Successful People

- *"Even if the chef has a good business head, his focus should be behind kitchen doors. A business partner should take care of everything in front of the kitchen doors."* — **Bobby Flay**

- *"Many people you think are individual achievers in fact have either a strong spousal partner over many years or a business partner who's either in the background, not given enough publicity or less egocentric."* — **Michael Eisner**

- *"In the past a leader was a boss. Today's leaders must be partners with their people.. they no longer can lead solely based on positional power."* — **Ken Blanchard**

- *"It is rare to find a business partner who is selfless. If you are lucky it happens once in a lifetime."* — **Michael Eisner**

- *"In this new wave of technology, you can't do it all yourself, you have to form alliances."* — **Carlos Slim Helu**

10 Great Tips

1. Make sure to share your business mission and vision with potential partners. Make sure all parties bring the same energy and enthusiasm to the table.

2. Each party must be honest and clear regarding their personal and professional goals and objectives.

3. Not only partners must choose the same destination, but they also need to select the same road to get there. As an example, if you want to open a restaurant and your goal is to be more profitable by building a franchise business in the future, you will be in big trouble if your partner is not interested in having a franchise and wants to have only one profitable restaurant.

4. All parties must clarify their needs and expectations from the partnership.

5. What are the strengths and weaknesses of each partner, and how do they complete each other?

6. Be clear as much as you can regarding responsibilities and roles each partner is going to handle.

7. Do not rush to create a partnership. Do not allow your energy and enthusiasm to blind you.

8. Have a solid agreement and write everything down to cover all matters not only when everything is going well but also when you face problems or even want to split.

9. Get legal advice to create a solid partnership agreement.

10. Keep in mind that a good friend or a family member is not necessarily a good business partner. Consider all professional and legal matters, even if you are creating a partnership with your family members or close friends.

Tools and Resources

1. Book: *The Partnership Charter: How To Start Out Right With Your New Business Partnership (or Fix The One You're In)*, by David Gage https://amzn.to/2ZsKv6g

2. Book: *Business Partnership Essentials: A Step-by-Step Action Plan for Succeeding in Business With a Partner, Second Edition* by Dorene Lehavi https://amzn.to/2KY0F3K

3. Book: *Cofounding The Right Way: A practical guide to successful business partnerships*, by Jana Nevrlka https://amzn.to/2zj2DFl

4. Book: *The Art of Strategic Partnering: Dancing with Elephants*, by Mark Sochan https://amzn.to/2KYi7F6

5. Book: *Partnernomics: The Art, Science, and Processes of Developing Successful Strategic Partnerships*, by Mark Brigman https://amzn.to/2zkkxYl

How to Terminate a Business Partnership

Why is it Important?

There are many reasons why you would want to terminate a business partnership. In some cases, it is essential to do so, while in other cases, it may become a legal necessity. Some key reasons why it may be necessary to terminate a business partnership include the following:

- When the term of the engagement has been completed.

- When one or more partners want to leave the business.

- In case a partner can't be legally part of the business.

- In case of an insolvency or a court order.

- In case a partner passes away.

Since a business is a legal entity, there are many issues involved in its termination. It is, therefore, important to take well-planned legal steps to terminate the partnership and ensure that all the dues and liabilities are correctly handled. In case this is not done correctly, prolonged litigation and innumerable legal and financial issues may arise.

Even if the business partnership is being terminated amicably, it is important to take proper legal advice so that the interests of all parties are looked after.

Quotes from Successful People

- *"The best partnerships aren't dependent on a mere common goal but on a shared path of equality, desire, and no small amount of passion."* — **Sarah MacLean**

- *"Perfect partners don't exist. Perfect conditions exist for a limited time in which partnerships express themselves best."* — **Wayne Rooney**

- *"An entrepreneur needs to know what they need, period. Then they need to find an investor who can build off whatever their weaknesses are— whether that's through money, strategic partnerships or knowledge."* — **Daymond John**

- *"If you like a person you say 'let's go into business together.' Man is a social animal after all, but such partnerships are fraught with danger."* — **Brian Tracy**

- *"I don't need to control anything. Even with romantic partnerships, I don't need to control anyone."* — **Cass McCombs**

10 Great Tips

1. Review your partnership agreement and consider all business and legal matters, including contracts, taxes, and assets.

2. What are the costs and benefits of splitting your partnership?

3. If something doesn't work out, you do not need to break up the partnership entirely. Sometimes it is better to change the level of a partnership. As an example, you can get more power in decision-making and implementation with more shares of the company.

4. Get legal advice if you want to dissolve or change the partnership.

5. If you do not have a partnership agreement, you should do your best to dissolve the partnership together. You can consult with an intermediary to find the best approach.

6. Communicate about all matters. Write down all important issues before talking to your lawyer and the partner.

7. Try to find a win-win solution. What are the most mutual desirable results?

8. If proper, notify your customers, suppliers, and other stakeholders regarding the changes in the business and partnership.

9. Do not burn all bridges and always be polite and honest. You may not be a business partner anymore, but you could be good friends.

10. Never talk badly about your former partner. This may ruin your own reputation first.

Tools and Resources

1. Small Business Administration - https://www.sba.gov/ - Understand the options available and the process involved by reading the material at this authoritative website.

2. Lawyers.com - http://lawyers.com/ - Ending a partnership can be complex, expensive, and draining. Take these important tips before proceeding.

3. Legal Zoom - https://www.legalzoom.com/ - There are many reasons for and methods of dissolving a partnership. Read this great resource to get educated on the subject.

4. Book: *Form a Partnership: The Complete Legal Guide*, by Denis Clifford, Ralph Warner https://amzn.to/2LtFfe2

5. Book: *The Founder's Dilemmas: Anticipating and Avoiding the Pitfalls That Can Sink a Startup*, by Noam Wasserman https://amzn.to/2NKWFpa

How to Manage Workplace Conflicts

Why is it Important?

Every relationship involves conflict. In some cases, the parties to the conflict may choose to underplay issues and adjust with each other, whereas in other cases, the conflict may erupt into open warfare and lead to endless trouble and strife. These two situations form the two ends of a conflict continuum with an endless list of situations in between.

Conflict is not always harmful. Consider a situation where two partners in a business have differing views on how to handle a situation. The conflicting views allow them to consider more aspects of the problem than they otherwise would, and if the differences are handled well, the final solution will be better than what it would have been without a free and frank discussion.

Practically every relationship involves some conflict at one stage or the other. Therefore, it is important to manage it sensibly and ensure that differences in ideas and ideology are not allowed to sour personal relationships. If this is ensured, businesses will prosper.

Quotes from Successful People

- *"A good manager doesn't try to eliminate conflict; he tries to keep it from wasting the energies of his people. If you're the boss and your people fight you openly when they think that you are wrong--that's healthy."* — **Robert Townsend**

- *"Conflict builds character. Crisis defines it."* — **Steven V Thulon**

- *"Listen first. Give your opponents a chance to talk. Let them finish. Do not resist, defend or debate. This only raises barriers. Try to build bridges of understanding."* — **Dale Carnegie**

- *"There are three ways of dealing with difference: domination, compromise, and integration. By domination only one side gets what it wants; by compromise neither side gets what it wants; by integration we find a way by which both sides may get what they wish."* — **Mary Parker Follett**

- *"The Law of Win/Win says, 'Let's not do it your way or my way; let's do it the best way.'"* — **Greg Anderson**

10 Great Tips

1. Create an environment in which all individuals can share their views and listen to each other respectfully.

2. Define the problem precisely.

3. Do not mix personal and professional issues since it completely distracts the discussion.

4. Focus on working behavior or professional mistakes instead of the person who does that. As an example, instead of blaming your employees to be complacent, you can emphasize ways that can improve productivity.

5. Try to conduct a reality check during the discussion.

6. Ask insightful questions to learn about involving parties' motivations.

7. Ask different sides to offer their suggestions and solutions.

8. Review different options with involving parties to find the best solution.

9. Develop an action plan to resolve the same issues if they happen again.

10. Review the actions taken and make corrections if necessary.

Tools and Resources

1. Book: *Conflict Management: A Practical Guide to Developing Negotiation Strategies*, by Barbara A. Budjac Corvette Ph.D https://amzn.to/2zKXsOx

2. Book: *Resolving Conflicts at Work: Ten Strategies for Everyone on the Job*, by Kenneth Cloke and Joan Goldsmith https://amzn.to/2NNBene

3. Book: *Crucial Conversations: Tools for Talking When Stakes Are High, Second Edition*, by Kerry Patterson, Joseph Grenny, Ron McMillan, Al Switzler https://amzn.to/2NKC58d

4. Book: *Influencer: The New Science of Leading Change, Second Edition*, by Joseph Grenny, Kerry Patterson, David Maxfield, Ron McMillan, Al Switzler https://amzn.to/34kzveT

5. Book: *The Anatomy of Peace: Resolving the Heart of Conflict*, by The Arbinger Institute https://amzn.to/2ZD8GmS

How to Secure Your Company's Information

Why is it Important?

It doesn't matter what kind of company you own. You are bound to have some form of sensitive data. It could be as simple as a name, an address, and an email ID or as sensitive as passwords or bank account details. In a society where the Internet reaches and affects all things, it is the company's duty to prevent misuse of the data they collect.

Data loss can also happen if you do not take good care of your computers. You may not get hacked; even common computer viruses can destroy all the data on your hard disks. Insider theft is also very common. Employees you fire can take away all your data and sell it to competitors. Small businesses are very vulnerable because they may not have the means to invest in strong protective measures.

Any loss of data can have serious repercussions for your business. You can lose the intellectual property on which your business is so critically dependent. Any loss of client data could expose you to lawsuits. Competitors could be trying to take away your clients and suppliers. All of this and more could happen because your business data is not adequately protected.

Quotes from Successful People

- *"Hackers find more success with organizations where employees are under appreciated, over worked and under paid. Why would anyone in an organization like that care enough to think twice before clicking on a phishing email?"* — **James Scott**

- *"Hardware is easy to protect: lock it in a room, chain it to a desk, or buy a spare. Information poses more of a problem. It can exist in more than one place; be transported halfway across the planet in seconds; and be stolen without your knowledge."* — **Bruce Schneier**

- *"If you think technology can solve your security problems, then you don't understand the problems and you don't understand the technology."* — **Bruce Schneier**

- *"The only truly secure system is one that is powered off, cast in a block of concrete and sealed in a lead-lined room with armed guards."* — **Gene Spafford**

- *"Passwords are like underwear: you don't let people see it, you should change it very often, and you shouldn't share it with strangers."* — **Chris Pirillo**

10 Great Tips

1. Develop both an on-site and online information backup system.

2. Create strong passwords for your computers and online accounts. Encrypt your sensitive data.

3. Ask your employees to sign a confidentiality agreement.

4. Update your security software regularly.

5. Get trained about the latest online threats.

6. Provide limited access to important data.

7. Train your employees to use and secure data.

8. Have an effective Internet policy. The policy will ensure that threats from the Internet are reduced and controlled, individuals work as they are expected to, and that no legal issues are emerging from their use of the Net.

9. Have regular checking to see if your information system works properly and securely.

10. Separate your personal and business accounts, such as emails and financial accounts.

Tools and Resources

1. Apptrana - https://apptrana.indusface.com/ - Continuously monitor the security of your computing infrastructure and take timely preventive action.

2. Book: *Cybersecurity Program Development for Business: The Essential Planning Guide*, by Chris Moschovitis
https://amzn.to/2NKgnRS

3. Book: *How to Measure Anything in Cybersecurity Risk 1st Edition*, by Douglas W. Hubbard, Richard Seiersen
https://amzn.to/2HF9EEK

4. Endpoint Protector - https://www.endpointprotector.com/ - A cross-platform tool that works across all popular operating

systems. Ensures that your workstations are safe and prevents compromise.

5. HTTPS Everywhere - https://www.eff.org/https-everywhere - HTTPS ensures secure web access, but all websites do not support it. Installing HTTPS everywhere forces websites to use the secure mode of data transfer to ensure your web activity is secure.

How to Analyze Your Business

Why is it Important?

If you are running a small business, you need to make sure that you are as efficient as possible and that every cent is spent in the most productive manner. One way to ensure this is by analyzing your business in-depth so that you understand what is important to you and your customers.

Many business owners try to copy what other people in a similar line of business are doing. While you could be copying their methods, you could also be copying their mistakes. If you sit down and analyze your business in-depth, however, you will come up with deep insights about how your business can be made unique and different.

The analysis also helps you understand market trends. You could be selling a great product and doing well, but research and analysis will tell you that a new technology is under development, which will disrupt the market. If you understand this, you can prepare yourself to take advantage of the development and emerge as a market leader.

Quotes from Successful People

- *"Data are becoming the new raw material of business."* — **Craig Mundie**

- *"The future belongs to those who see possibilities before they become obvious."* — **John Scully**

- *"Data is the new currency, and it's the medium of exchange between consumers and marketers."* — **Lisa Utzschneider**

- *"The most valuable commodity I know of is information."* — **Gordon Gekko**

- *"An organization's ability to learn, and translate that learning into action rapidly, is the ultimate competitive advantage."* — **Jack Welch**

10 Great Tips

1. The success and growth of a small business often depend on several internal and external factors. A careful analysis of all such factors is essential to ensure that you are able to assess the impact of these factors on your marketing efforts.

2. Situational analysis involves a thorough analysis of all operations, conditions, and other factors that are currently affecting your business. The best part about doing this kind of in-depth investigation of your business is that it will reveal other hidden factors that might be important in the future.

3. It is very important to know what you are looking for in business analysis. Are you trying to check your business performance? Are you going to get a complete view of the external environment you are operating in?

4. Your analysis should be both quantitative to review your business performance, such as the number of customers, and qualitative to learn the causes of increasing or decreasing the rate of your customers.

5. 5Cs analysis is a great framework to analyze 5Cs (Company, Customers, Competitors, Collaborators, Climate of the market)

6. The followings are some of the questions that you should ask during 5Cs analysis:

    a. What are the strengths and weaknesses of your company?

  b. Which of your 5 Ps do your customers like the most (product/pricing/placement/promotions/people)?

  c. Which of your competitors are doing better than you are? Why are they so good?

  d. Who are your collaborators? How can you get referrals from them?

  e. What are the new trends, laws, and technologies in your industry?

7. Reviewing your financial statements, such as profit and loss and balance sheet, is another way to review your business.

8. GAP analysis is another way by which you draw a table with three columns. The first column is your current situation, the second column is your desired situation, and the third one is how you are planning to reach your goals.

9. SWOT analysis is another tool by which you write down your company's strengths and weaknesses and also opportunities and threats that you face.

10. Keep in mind that business analysis should be down at least twice a year to give you a better understanding of your business situation.

Tools and Resources

1. Wrike - www.wrike.com - A business analysis and project management tool used by many professionals.

2. Enterprise Architect - http://www.sparxsystems.com/products/ea/ - Manage the entire life cycle for your business and IT systems and build robust products. Keep track of all high-level requirements and ensure your business scales up efficiently.

3. Case Spec - http://visualtracespec.com/ - Analyze and grow your business with a focus on products, test cases, bugs, issues, and customer requirements. Share data across the enterprise and use predefined as well as customized reports to keep track of business developments.

4. Book: *Business Analysis for Practitioners: A Practice Guide*, by Project Management Institute https://amzn.to/2ZLuxVc

5. Book: *Seven Steps to Mastering Business Analysis*, by Barbara Carkenord https://amzn.to/2Lj129r

How to Manage Your Business Remotely

Why is it Important?

Let's face it. If you are going to be sitting in one office and trying to run your business all the time, you will not have much spare time to do anything else. A well-run business must run on auto most of the time. Procedures and rules must be in place to ensure that most activity takes place routinely and that the business owners and managers are left free to think about how to improve the product and increase the range of services being offered.

If you want to be able to manage your business remotely, a few things must be implemented. The first of these is good work ethics and standard operating procedures (SOPs). Setting good SOPs helps your employees make the appropriate decisions when you are not available to guide them. Once this is achieved, you can pay attention to other issues, such as diversifying your business and developing new products.

Effective business leaders also stay abreast of modern technology. This helps them manage their business remotely. They can be with clients or contractors on the other side of the globe and yet be in touch with every aspect of their business.

Quotes from Successful People

- *"People today really value workplace flexibility and remote work because it allows them to focus their energies on work and life as opposed to commuting or other complications due to geography."* — **Ken Matos**

- *"We like to give people the freedom to work where they want, safe in the knowledge that they have the drive and expertise to perform excellently, whether they [are] at their desk or in their kitchen. Yours truly has never worked out of an office, and never will."* — **Richard Branson**

- *"We need to take a more flexible approach to both the workplace and the work we do; one that provides us both the physical and cognitive space to harness the incredible power, insight and experience we offer, but focused not on the individual processes but instead on the overall outcomes our organizations are seeking to achieve."* — **David Coplin**

- *"Telecommuting, one of many forms of work-life flexibility, should no longer be viewed as a nice-to-have, optional perk mostly used by working moms. These common stereotypes don't match reality—allowing employees to work remotely is a core business strategy today... We need to de-parent, de-gender, and de-age the perception of the flexible worker."* — **Cali Williams Yost**

- *"Technology now allows people to connect anytime, anywhere, to anyone in the world, from almost any device. This is dramatically changing the way people work, facilitating 24/7 collaboration with colleagues who are dispersed across time zones, countries, and continents."* — **Michael Dell**

10 Great Tips

1. Develop a system for your business that does not rely on one person completely. With this system, employees know their tasks, and all main working procedures are explicit.

2. Have an effective training program so that you can train your employees and delegate some of your tasks to them.

3. Empower your employees to make low-risk decisions if needed.

4. Define parameters and variables to review your employees' performance. Keep in mind that quality, quantity, and time are the three important elements of performance management.

5. Use different online tools and applications to manage your business remotely.

6. Have an office assistant to conduct office jobs for you if needed.

7. Use video or voice conferencing to continue your regular meetings with your staff.

8. Set surveillance cameras to check out your business environment remotely.

9. Test your employees to see how they perform when you are out. This can be done, for example, by sending fake customers, phone inquiries, and testing online security measures.

10. Do not completely rely on the remote management system. Visit your business once a while.

Tools and Resources

1. Slack - https://slack.com/ - Build a virtual office and work from anywhere. Slack ensures that your team works together even though they may be geographically separated.

2. EveryTimeZone - https://everytimezone.com/ - If your remote teams are scattered in different time zones and you want to find a time when everyone can be online together, EveryTimeZone is the tool to use. Use this great visual tool to coordinate with your business partners remotely.

3. Asana - https://asana.com/ - Coordinate all your team and business tasks even though you all are in remote locations. Ensure that no work is lost sight of and everything comes together when it is due.

4. Quip - https://quip.com/ - This very useful tool from Salesforce starts by looking like a document sharing tool. As you begin using it, you find it is a fantastic notification and collaboration tool too. It is ideal for people running their businesses remotely.

5. LastPass - https://www.lastpass.com/ - When your teams work remotely, there can be many accounts and passwords to manage. This itself can be a major challenge. LastPass gets rid of the complexity and gives every user a single sign-on and controls access to accounts you specify.

How to Smooth Your Business Operation

Why is it Important?

If every day of running your business is spent firefighting, you will not be able to achieve very much. A successful business must be able to run on autopilot for most routine activities, leaving the managers free to work on managing relations with clients, looking out for new business opportunities, and expanding the product portfolio.

Smooth business operations mean that your workflow and inventory management are well-coordinated, your employees are well trained and equipped to produce your goods without having to be monitored continuously, and the quality of your products and services is so good that customer complaints are minimized.

If you are able to get your business to such a stable state of operations, you will be able to predict your activities and plan for them in time. There will be no last-minute running around and panic. You will be able to plan for future events and anticipate your business needs. In short, smooth business operations mean that the business is under control and progressing well.

Quotes from Successful People

- *"The first rule of any technology used in a business is that automation applied to an efficient operation will magnify the efficiency. The second is that automation applied to an inefficient operation will magnify the inefficiency."* — **Bill Gates**

- *"While successful leaders address all four areas, the best leaders always start with why followed very closely by who. Then, and only then, do they work on the design of what and how."* — **Mike Myatt**

- *"Commitment without understanding is a liability."* — **Oliver Wight**

- *"There is nothing so useless as doing efficiently that which should not be done at all."* — **Peter F. Drucker**

- *"Process improvement programs are like teaching people how to fish. Strategy maps and scorecards teach people where to fish."* — **Robert S. Kaplan**

10 Great Tips

1. Develop a system for your business. The system must include working procedures in different divisions of your business.

2. Create an operation manual so that your employees know about their job descriptions, your business standards, and other important matters.

3. Improve your business manual regularly. Involve employees in adding new techniques and materials to improve your working procedures.

4. Have regular meetings with your staff to see how to make the business operation smoother. Always encourage your employees to share their opinions.

5. Train your employees and delegate tasks so that they do not need to rely on you in all matters.

6. Review top businesses in your industry and see how they manage their operations.

7. You should have both internal and external effective business operations. How is your relationship with your suppliers, vendors, and collaborators? How can you make more effective and efficient working relationships and business procedures with them?

8. Define important elements of your business operation, such as customer order processing time, answering phone time, employee punctuality, quality of your products and services, and customer satisfaction.

9. Review important operation elements every three months to see how your business operation is performing.

10. Do not try to fix and improve all issues at the same time. Start from the main one and go to the others.

Tools and Resources

1. iDoneThis - https://home.idonethis.com/- Ensure your teams work smoothly by using a good reporting tool that allows team members to share the work they have done and keep everyone in sync. iDoneThis is great at this.

2. Harvest - https://www.getharvest.com/ - Keep track of time. Harvest keeps your projects running smoothly by keeping track of your teams, their time use, and what they have achieved. Harvest collects data about how your teams work and creates insightful reports.

3. Glip - https://glip.com/ - Keep your business running smoothly with Glip—manage tasks, share files and calendars, record your chat sessions, and empower your teams to keep your business running like a well-oiled machine.

4. Trello - https://trello.com - Eliminate chaos and uncertainty from your projects by using Trello. This productivity tool allows you to assign tasks to individuals or teams, assign deadlines, and track progress so that your projects run smoothly, and any deviations are corrected early.

5. PandaDoc - https://www.pandadoc.com/ - PandaDoc document management solution cuts out the paperwork from your documents and lets you go truly digital. Create, dispatch, and track documents; add digital signatures, and monitor responses from an easy-to-use interface.

How to Deal with Legal Issues in Your Business

Why is it Important?

There are always legal issues that may affect your business. You could get into disputes with customers, contractors, or suppliers; you could be planning to expand into other markets in other countries, and there could be issues with inspectors and auditors. In most cases, a developing legal issue is like a weed in a garden. It starts small, but if not controlled in time, it has the potential to grow out of control and take over the landscape.

Most small-business owners are forced to wear many hats, but they are seldom able to do justice to a legal hat because they may not have the knowledge to do so. In such situations, the business must invest in the services of a competent attorney right from the beginning. A good lawyer on your team will be able to vet your agreements and contracts and alert you to issues that could go against your interests later. Even such simple and routine activities as hiring and termination have several legal issues associated with them. You could be sued by an employee who feels aggrieved by your policies or actions. Once this starts, it could require a lot of your time and resources.

Therefore, it is important to ensure that your legal issues are dealt with correctly in time when they are still small and can be managed. If you do not resolve issues in the early stages, they may become very difficult to manage as they get older and more complicated.

Quotes from Successful People

- *"The type of person you are is usually reflected in your business. To improve your business, first improve yourself."* — **Idowu Koyenikan**

- *"Hire character. Train skill."* — **Peter Schutz**

59

- *"Relationships are the only thing that matter in business in life."* — **Jerry Weintraub**

- *"No man suffers injustice without learning, vaguely but surely, what justice is."* — **Isaac Rosenfeld**

- *"It is an immutable law in business that words are words, explanations are explanations, promises are promises but only performance is reality."* — **Harold Geneen**

10 Great Tips

1. Learn about all legal matters that you may face, such as business registration, employee hiring and management, and trademarks.

2. Hire a great lawyer to get advice regarding important matters.

3. Try to have agreements in all business matters, such as dealing with suppliers and employees.

4. Update yourself about the new laws and regulations in your industry.

5. It is a good idea to review all your legal documents and matters at least once a year.

6. Be proactive in facing legal issues. Prevention is always better than reaction.

7. Educate your employees regarding legal issues.

8. Ask your lawyer to review your business and employment policies.

9. If you have businesses in different locations, always check local laws and regulations.

10. Always follow the law. Keep in mind that sooner or later cheaters will be in trouble.

Tools and Resources

1. NOLO - https://www.nolo.com/ - Get legal advice and large numbers of do-it-yourself forms and legal documents at NOLO. Use the same resource to find a lawyer specially qualified in whichever domain you need help in.

2. Rocket Lawyer - https://www.rocketlawyer.com/ - Simplify legal issues with Rocket Lawyer. Start with ready-to-use documents and articles and switch to a real lawyer whenever you need one.

3. DocuSign - https://www.docusign.com/ - Getting legal documents and agreements signed with your clients and business partners is easier than ever before. DocuSign creates legally enforceable documents that allow you to focus on your business rather than on the documentation.

4. Trademarkia - https://www.trademarkia.com/ - Check for trademarks, patents, domain names, and logos for free using this great resource.

5. LawDepot - https://www.lawdepot.com - Create legal documents online, customize them the way you want, and download them all ready to go. You can customize the document to the country you want.

How to Provide High-Quality Service

Why is it Important?

It is a common saying in management that measurements are the backbone of efficiency. Numerous studies have proven this to be correct, and all successful businesses have devised detailed ways to measure all their important parameters. One key parameter that all successful businesses measure is the quality of their services.

It is well-known that it costs you much more to acquire a new customer than to retain one. The most important means of retaining a customer is by ensuring high-quality service. Businesses realize that sometimes delivery will be late and that the goods you sell will fail. This can happen even in the best governed and managed companies. What is important is how you react after a failure, or bad service episode occurs.

Very often, managers feel their business is doing well, and sales are booming. If they took care to measure the quality of their service, however, they would find out that the number of repeat customers is reducing, and that there are several adverse comments about their quality of service. With the Internet touching us all and with social media becoming so powerful, it is only a matter of time before a decline in the quality of service translates into a decline in sales and reputation.

All of this goes to show that as a business owner/manager, you need to measure how good is the quality of service you provide your customers. Once you lose customers, it is very difficult to win them back again.

Quotes from Successful People

- *"Well done is better than well said."* — **Benjamin Franklin**

- *"Excellence is an art won by training and habituation."* — **Aristotle**

- *"If we don't take care of our customers, someone else will."* — **Edgar Mitchell**

- *"There are no traffic jams along the extra mile."* — **Roger Staubach**

- *"Quality in a service or product is not what you put into it. It is what the client or customer gets out of it."* — **Peter Drucker**

10 Great Tips

1. Find out the requirements to conduct a great service. That may include on-time delivery, responsiveness, and availability.

2. Imagine you are going to use your services. What are the most important factors for you?

3. Compare your service with top players in your industry. What can you learn from them?

4. Learn about your competitors and provide better service than they do. Check review websites to see what their customers have written about them.

5. Learn about your customer expectations. Customers call your service high quality if you go beyond their expectations.

6. Get feedback from your customers to see how you can improve your service.

7. Ask your customers to see if they refer you to their friends and families. Find out why they do or do not.

8. Have great connections with related businesses so that you can refer them to your customers. Try to be a one-stop place for your customers' questions and needs.

9. Review your business procedures to determine how to improve them.

10. Promise less, deliver more.

Tools and Resources

1. Mention - https://mention.com/en/ - Know what your customers are saying about you, your competitors, and your products. Quickly catch errors in service before they have time to go viral.

2. SurveyMonkey - https://www.surveymonkey.com - Build a questionnaire using Survey Monkey. Mail your survey to customers and get a meaningful analysis of results.

3. Google Alerts - https://www.google.com/alerts - Monitor the Internet to know what people say about you, your brand, your website, and practically anything else. Best of all, it's completely free!

4. Book: *The Toyota Way to Service Excellence: Lean Transformation in Service Organizations,* by Jeffrey K. Liker, Karyn Ross https://amzn.to/2PCfe1k

5. Book: *Service Operations Management: Improving Service Delivery (4th Edition),* by Robert Johnston, Graham Clark, Michael Shulver https://amzn.to/2ZKZEjH

How to Productize Your Service

Why is it Important?

Many business owners who run service companies find that they run into limitations when they try to expand. The problem lies in the nature of the service industry. Since there are so few tangibles, the offerings can often be unclear and nebulous. All your competitors offer the same service, and every one offers prospective clients the moon. There seems to be no way to differentiate between different service providers.

There is one way that can ensure that you stand out from the crowd. This is by productizing your service. When you productize your service, you offer your clients a complete package that is tailor-made for them. Every client is different, and therefore the product you offer has to be different too. In this manner, service firms can put together a large array of services that build on some core capabilities.

When these products are offered on your website, and clear pricing is defined, your prospective clients have a wider array of services to choose from. They are able to understand your offerings with greater clarity and can determine exactly what they will be required to pay. This results in sales lead where the client is not exploring your services but is already primed to buy.

Quotes from Successful People

- *"To give real service you must add something which cannot be bought or measured with money, and that is sincerity and integrity."* — **Douglas Adams**

- *"Perfection is not attainable, but if we chase perfection we can catch excellence."* — **Vince Lombardi**

- *"You are what you do, not what you say you'll do."* — **C.G. Jung**

- *"Here is a powerful yet simple rule. Always give people more than they expect to get."* — **Nelson Boswell**

- *"People expect good service but few are willing to give it."* — **Robert Gately**

10 Great Tips

1. If you provide a service, you can make it more understandable and tangible for your customers by productizing it.

2. Productizing means developing standards by which your customers exactly know what they get by hiring you. This may build more trust and reduces the customer's risks.

3. One of the best productization approaches is to create different service packages that show what service you offer, the fees, your customers' results, and other terms and conditions.

4. To productize your service, you must find out the most common and recurring needs of your customers.

5. Categorize your services based on the time, information, and other resources you provide to solve the customer's needs

6. Set a price for each category. Test your pricing options before mass marketing.

7. Add your service packages to your website and other marketing channels.

8. Provide free consultation or an assessment session to learn more about the customer's needs before offering a specific service package.

9. Get feedback from your customers and optimize your service packages.

10. Be flexible and provide an option for customers who do not want to use your packages and want to pay as they go.

Tools and Resources

1. InVision - https://www.invisionapp.com/ - Build a complete mockup of your desired website without any coding. Get quick feedback and ensure glitch-free operations from day one.

2. SweetProcess - https://www.sweetprocess.com/ - Document all your repetitive tasks and create standard operating procedures so that your people know exactly how they are to work. Works well for manufacturing as well as service-oriented businesses.

3. Scoro - https://www.scoro.com/ - Put structure in your work and ensure your teams stay in synch. Comprehensive reports on all aspects of your business help you keep track of what's important.

4. Toggl - https://toggl.com/ - Keep track of the time you or your team members spend on tasks. A great tool for those who use freelancers. Standard time measurements and billing ensure accuracy and accountability.

5. Bitrix 24 - https://www.bitrix24.com/ - Handle your mail in time to ensure you do not overlook anything critical. Bitrix 24 makes mail handling a part of your SOPs so that it becomes an automatic activity. As you grow, Bitrix 24 expands its offerings to give you social media monitoring and other capabilities.

How to Develop a System for Your Business

Why is it Important?

If you sit down and analyze your business activities, you will probably find that they can be grouped into routine and predictable activities or actions that are the result of some exceptions or unusual situations. Business owners or managers will always be required to devote their time and effort to deal with the unusual or emergency situations, but they can ensure that routine activity is taken care of by a well-settled system within their business workflow.

Take a situation where your business relies on a number of subcontractors to produce a finished product. If the business is well organized, then there will be well-established procedures to order components in time and to check the quality of what is being received and produced. Businesses that do not have well-established systems in place will be forever firefighting.

Putting systems in place ensures that all foreseeable activities are programmed, and that important issues are all taken care of. You are then left free to take care of the exceptions and the issues that cannot be solved without your intervention.

Quotes from Successful People

- *"In order for any business to succeed, it must first become a system so that the business functions exactly the same way every time down to the last detail."* — **Rick Harshaw**

- *"The two most important lessons that today's quality practitioners can learn from W. Edwards Deming and the total quality management movement of the 1980s are that quality equals process, and that everything is a process. Managing an organization's processes is crucial to ensuring its quality systems."* — **Ronald M. Cordes**

- *"If you can't describe what you are doing as a process, you don't know what you're doing."* — **W. Edwards Deming**

- *"The entrepreneurial perspective views business as a network of seamlessly integrated components, each contributing to some larger pattern that comes together in such a way as to produce a specifically planned result, a systematic way of doing business."* — **Michael Gerber**

- *"Systems help us to move forward, to go as far as we possibly can. They enable us to work faster, smarter, and more strategically. A good system eliminates waste, while it also anticipates and removes obstacles. To get the most out of systems, you have to make them a lifestyle not a one-off deal. They must become ingrained in your routine."* — **John Maxwell**

10 Great Tips

1. A business system is a framework that defines your important working procedures, responsibilities of your employees, and resources needed in different sections of your business.

2. An effective business system is clear, understandable, documented, flexible, and scalable. Keep in mind that if you have an effective system for your business, you do not need to supervise your employees one by one. Instead, you control your system and the results of your working procedures.

3. Start by defining your working processes in different areas, such as sales, marketing, hiring, and inventory management.

4. See which activities give you the most results and ask your employees to write them down as well.

5. Review top businesses in your industry to determine how their systems work.

6. Have regular meetings with your staff and finalize your working procedures.

7. Write down job descriptions, required skills, and resources needed to complete each working process successfully.

8. Set your working standards and results in terms of quality, quantity, and time to measure the performance of each activity.

9. Create a working manual accessible by all your employees to answer their questions and get feedback from them.

10. Review your business system regularly and improve it.

Tools and Resources

1. Wrike - https://wrike.com/ - Use Wrike to manage your projects and keep your business running smoothly. Start with a free plan and upgrade as required.

2. Video Conference - https://www.join.me/ - Have you begun using videoconferencing to stay in touch with your clients and business partners? Set up a schedule to stay in regular touch and smooth your business operations.

3. Deputy - https://www.deputy.com/ - Set up good HR systems to manage your staff and your hiring procedures. You can try for free and upgrade to a paid version when you find it useful.

4. Wave - https://www.waveapps.com/ - Are your accounting systems set up completely? If in doubt, check out Wave. It's an accounting system built for start-ups and will grow as your needs increase.

5. Worketc. - https://www.worketc.com/ - A pioneer in "all in one" business tools, Worketc comes with all the functionality that a small business would ever need.

How to Set Your Business Goals and Achieve Them

Why is it Important?

As a business owner, you always want efficiency and good plan execution. It can often happen, however, that you get so caught up in the day-to-day activities of running your business that you lose sight of the big picture and neglect planning for the future. This can be avoided by realistic and challenging goal-setting activity. If you set up clearly defined goals and work toward achieving these goals, your business will gain in the following ways:

- You will have a clearly defined road map for your work.

- You will be able to identify areas where you are lagging and take timely corrective actions.

- The collaboration and teamwork in your work environment will improve.

- All your employees will understand your priorities and will know where to direct their energies.

To set realistic business goals, you need to sit down with your key employees and partners and decide the direction your business needs to take. Based on the points that emerge, you can decide a few actionable points to set as your targets. Periodically take feedback to see if you are working toward the goals and make necessary course corrections. Working in this manner will ensure that your business is aligned with your long-term vision.

Quotes from Successful People

- *"If you want to be happy, set a goal that commands your thoughts, liberates your energy and inspires your hopes."* — **Andrew Carnegie**

- *"Our goals can only be reached through a vehicle of a plan, in which we must fervently believe, and upon which we must vigorously act. There is no other route to success."* — **Pablo Picasso**

- *"The entrepreneur is essentially a visualizer and actualizer . . . He can visualize something, and when he visualizes it he sees exactly how to make it happen."* — **Robert L. Schwartz**

- *"A goal properly set is halfway reached."* — **Zig Ziglar**

- *"The trouble with not having a goal is that you can spend your life running up and down the field and never score."* — **Bill Copeland**

10 Great Tips

1. You should have both long- and short-term goals for your business.

2. Long-term goals are usually three, five, or ten years, and they must be based on the mission and vision of your business.

3. Break down your big goals and dreams to short-term achievable goals and actions.

4. Involve your employees in setting your goals. This way, they have part ownership of the decision and get more motivated to achieve goals.

5. Apple SMART rule in defining your short-term goals. Your short-term goals must be:

   a. Specific: You must focus and define your goals in detail.

   b. Measurable: You must assign a number to your goal and be able to measure your success or failure in achieving them. As an example, adding fifty more customers per month is a measurable goal.

   c. Action-oriented: You should identify the actions needed to achieve your goals and assign them to your employees.

   d. Realistic: Your goals must be realistic, based on your current business situation and the resources you have to achieve them.

   e. Time Specific: Goals without a deadline are just dreams. Set a timetable to achieve your goals. As an example, you are going to get fifty new customers within the next three months.

6. Motivation, responsibility, and consistency are the three main requirements to achieve your goals.

7. Have regular meetings with your employees and review your goals and business performance.

8. Be flexible and change your goals based on internal and external business environment changes. Remember the 5Cs (Company, Customer, Competitors, Climate of the market).

9. Reward yourself and your employees who do their best to help the business achieve its goals.

10. Prioritize your goals and start with the most important ones. Make sure your goals do not have conflicts with each other.

Tools and Resources

1. Any Do - https://www.any.do/ - A very simple interface, easy-to-use, and efficient goal managing and reminder tool. Create lists for any category of jobs, track individual activities, and increase efficiency.

2. WunderList - https://www.wunderlist.com/ - Synchronize your goals and related activity across every device you use so that you can track your tasks and progress from anywhere. Manage unlimited projects and activities.

3. To Do - https://todo.microsoft.com/ - To Do takes managing lists and goals one step forward. It sees your leftover tasks from previous days and gives you suggestions on what you can accomplish additionally. Native integration with Microsoft Office and great security features are additional attractions for this great app.

4. Book: *Free to Focus: A Total Productivity System to Achieve More by Doing Less*, by Michael Hyatt https://amzn.to/34keukP

5. Book: *Principles: Life and Work*, by Ray Dalio https://amzn.to/2LguJYp

How to Make Effective Task lists

Why is it Important?

Small-business owners do not have large teams of specialist staff members to do their work. Very often, the business owner has to take on many different tasks. This may involve setting priorities and handling stress and work pressure.

Having a task list ensures you take a holistic look at your pending work and are able to prioritize. The time you have is limited, and unless you work to a plan, you can miss out on the really important activities. If you work without a list, you will end up doing what first comes to the mind or is more interesting and lose sight (or put off) doing something that is difficult or boring. A prioritized list ensures this does not happen.

Making a list also helps you delegate your work better. You can sort the list into tasks that you can give to an assistant or outsource. This allows you to focus on your core competencies and what you are good at. Try working with a list and see the difference it makes in your efficiency.

Quotes from Successful People

- *"Sometimes our stop-doing list needs to be bigger than our to-do list."* — **Patti Digh**

- *"Rename your 'To-Do' list to your 'Opportunities' list. Each day is a treasure chest filled with limitless opportunities; take joy in checking many off your list."* — **Steve Maraboli**

- *"Each day I will accomplish one thing on my to do list."* — **Lailah Gifty Akita**

- *"Checking items off a to-do list doesn't determine progress; focusing on your priorities is what counts."* — **Frank Sonnenberg**

- *"The only thing more important than your to-do list is your to-be list. The only thing more important than your to-be list is to be."* — **Alan Cohen**

10 Great Tips

1. You should have two types of lists—a master list that you can write once a week and a daily to-do list for your daily activities.

2. Every Sunday, try to find a quiet place and write down whatever comes to your mind for both personal and professional tasks that need to be done next week. Do not forget to add a deadline for each task.

3. Your master list can work as a reference for your daily to-do lists, although you may add un-forecasted tasks to your daily list as well.

4. Every day based on your master list and your work, write the top five tasks that you need to complete. This could be your daily task list.

5. Do not make a big list. Start with five important ones and add other items one by one if you finish the first five. This way, you will be less stressed and feel more productive.

6. Some management gurus even recommend writing down only the most important thing that you need to do daily and add other items one by one.

7. You can make your daily list at the end of each day for the next day. This way, when you get home, you already know that your mind is free from all professional things, and you can concentrate more on your family and personal activities.

8. Be flexible! There are always unpredictable things that may happen. Do not make a very tight, back-to-back schedule for yourself.

9. Be realistic! Do not try to accomplish many things in a very short period of time. Quality is much important than quantity.

10. Use mobile apps or task management software to access your lists whenever you want and also get reminders about your important tasks.

Tools and Resources

1. Wunderlist - https://www.wunderlist.com/ - Recently bought over by Microsoft, Wunderlist is easy to use and can

handle everything from basic worklists to business management. Available for iOS, Android, and your laptop.

2. Todoist - https://todoist.com/ - Keep all your to-do lists in one place, synchronize across devices, and even add to lists when you are offline. Create tasks, subtasks, and dependencies all in the free version. Upgrade to paid if you need advanced features.

3. Trello - https://trello.com/ - Create job cards and lists and drag and drop tasks between lists. Color-coded tasks help you organize lists better and automatically switch to calendar view to see how you are doing for time.

4. ToodleDo - https://www.toodledo.com/ - Organize your work, schedule, habits, and life with ToodleDo. Most users swear by it. Synch all your tasks across the iOS, Android, and web platforms.

5. Any.do - https://www.any.do/ - Beautifully organized, easy to use, and extremely functional, Any.do can change the way you work and increase your efficiency. Easy synch with third-party calendar applications, smartwatches, and Siri and Alexa.

How to Develop a Budget for Your Business

Why is it Important?

When you start working on your small business, it is extremely important to begin with a reasonably accurate estimate of your budget. You do not want to be like the contractor who could only build half a bridge. There are a certain number of activities that you must accomplish. If you do not budget for these, you will jeopardize your business and your capital.

The lack of budgeting may cause two situations: (1) you could run short of money because you have not prioritized your expenses, and (2) you may not be spending adequately to support and grow the business. Either condition is harmful to the growth of your business.

It is also important for small-business owners to understand the basics of accounting. Unless they take the time to learn this, they will be working on instinct and gut feeling. Therefore, while you may want to focus on the operational aspects, you must take time to budget your expenses, anticipate future expenses, calculate revenues, and control expenditure. The survival of your business depends on this.

Quotes from Successful People

- *"Budgeting has only one rule: Do not go over budget."* — **Leslie Tayne**

- *"A budget tells us what we can't afford, but it doesn't keep us from buying it."* — **William Feather**

- *"The budget is not just a collection of numbers, but an expression of our values and aspirations."* — **Jacob Lew**

- *"Beware of little expenses. A small leak will sink a great ship."* — **Benjamin Franklin**

- *"I wasn't a financial pro, and I paid the price."* — **Ruth Handler**

10 Great Tips

1. A budget is a great tool in business planning and reviewing performance, controlling business expenses, and fulfilling your financial commitments.

2. Take your time to create a realistic and comprehensive budget.

3. Collect historical or your industry information regarding potential sales, revenue, and expenses. If you already have a business, you can get the information for the last year and revise it based on current conditions.

4. Three main components of a budget:

   a. Projected cash flow (monthly cash flow)

    b. Business Costs (fixed, variable, one-time spends)

    c. Revenue (based on your sales history and your forecast)

5. Fixed costs are expenses that stay the same and are not related to the sales volume, such as rent and insurance.

6. Variable costs are directly related to the sales volume, such as raw material expenses and shipping expenses.

7. Be flexible and adjust your budget based on unpredicted changes.

8. Review your budget regularly. A budget can be a great tool to determine the differences between forecasted and actual revenue and expenses.

9. Compare your yearly budgets to see the trends in your business.

10. Involve the right people, such as managers and key employees, in developing the budget. It is also a good idea to get a second opinion from your business accountant and consultant.

Tools and Resources

1. Scoro - https://www.scoro.com/ - Budgeting software that comes with a host of tools that take functionality beyond basic budgeting. Manage your company finances with Scoro.

2. Centage - http://www.centage.com/ - Combine enterprise budgeting with financial reporting and forecasting. Get a comprehensive solution with Centage.

3. Prophix - http://www.prophix.com/ - An all-in-one solution for all your budgeting, forecasting, reporting, and cash flow management needs.

4. Float - http://floatapp.com/ - Float combines budgeting with forecasting and offers attractive, easy-to-use, and understandable visual reporting functions. A very well-designed visual interface is its USP.

5. Planguru - http://www.planguru.com/ - Planguru is simpler in coverage and use as compared with more complex solutions, but this is exactly what most small businesses require.

How to Identify and Manage Your Business Risks

Why is it Important?

Small businesses face a large number of risks. The effect of any adverse event is greater on a small business because resources are limited, and even a small shock can hurt the business. Many small businesses work with very limited human resources. This also reduces their capacity to handle risks.

In today's business environment, data loss is a major threat. This can take place due to a technical failure or human error. In either case, this could have very major consequences on the survivability of your business.

There are a number of physical risks that your business could be facing. Think about fire, flood, and security-related threats. Have you taken adequate precautions against these threats? Besides physical risks, there are other risks, such as technology risks, legal risks, and human risks, that need to be considered.

Business owners need to be aware of these and many other risks that could affect them. If they can anticipate them and take timely corrective action, then the effect of the event (if it were to occur) would be controlled to quite a degree.

Quotes from Successful People

- *"I knew that if I failed I wouldn't regret that, but I knew the one thing I might regret is not trying."* — **Jeff Bezos**

- *"If you are not in touch with your intuition, you cannot be successful. Data is great. But sometimes, even when you have all the data in the world, if you don't follow your gut, you won't discover the true potential and be able to recognize critical opportunities."* — **Arianna Huffington**

- *"By establishing milestones, gates, and questions along the way, you're ensuring that you're being smart about the risks you're taking. And as hard as it is, you've got to be ready to say, "We are stopping."* — **Ina Kamenz**

- *"You have to [take risks] if you're going to innovate and revolutionize anything with an organization. In fact, your tolerance for risk is directly related to how successful you can be and that tolerance is worth challenging."* — **Ginna Raahauge**

- *"The only thing worse than starting something and failing is not starting something."* — **Seth Godin**

10 Great Tips

1. Identifying, preventing, and managing risks, which is called risk management, is one of the saviors for your business.

2. List all your important business procedures that without them your business stops working.

3. Find out all requirements, such as employees, tools, information, and materials, that you need to run your main business procedures.

4. Think about what kinds of incidents that may happen to business procedures and the required elements that may have a negative effect on the processes, such as losing information, effective employees, power supply, and lack of having raw materials.

5. Asking the following questions may help you to identify your business risks:

   a. What if we have no Internet connection?

   b. What if we lose our information?

c. What if my manager or an effective employee cannot come to work or quit?

d. What if our suppliers cannot provide material on time?

6. Develop an action plan to prevent and deal with all potential incidents. It is recommended to have a risk management manual, including potential risks and how to manage them.

7. Consult with your lawyer, accountant, business coach, and other related experts to determine how to identify and manage business risks.

8. Check out your industry news to learn about new rules, technological trends, and other external environmental factors that may affect your business.

9. Cross-training your employees, having a solid knowledge management system, backing up your important information, having different insurance, having more than one supplier, and checking all safety matters are some of the actions that may prevent your business risks.

10. Review your risk management plan and improve it constantly.

Tools and Resources

1. Resolver - https://www.resolver.com/ - A single-source solution to manage business risk, corporate security, and improve business resilience. Resolver allows data sharing across the company to ensure all stakeholders are kept informed of the risks the business is dealing with.

2. Standard Fusion - https://www.standardfusion.com/ - Identify and analyze risks that your business could be facing. Ensure that your business is truly compliant and protected at all times.

3. Diligent - https://diligent.com/ - Diligent Board Portal allows company board members to probe deeper into risks, ask better questions, and understand the overall risk environment better. Truly a tool focused on big-ticket thinking.

4. OnSpring - https://www.onspring.com/solutions/risk-management-software - OnSpring risk management solutions help you identify risks early and take prompt and verifiable corrective action.

5. Book: *Principles of Risk Management and Insurance*, by George E. Rejda and Michael McNamara https://amzn.to/2LiWNt6

How to Get More Motivated at Work

Why is it Important?

Most small-business owners are highly motivated people who have faith in their capacity to create and market great products. With the difficulties that small businesses may face, however, it is easy for some owners to become less motivated. In fact, it has been said that nearly 80 percent of small businesses may not be able to survive beyond four to five years.

The important point is that 20 percent do survive and go on to become successful. This statistic alone should encourage small-business owners to look for the important ingredient that ensures success. The difference lies in the motivation of the owners and in their capacity to generate enthusiasm in their team members.

Being motivated also ensures that once you find out what does not work, you have the fire in you to change course and try alternate methods of working. Maybe you change your marketing methods, maybe you change the area you are in, or maybe you change the product itself. A motivated business person will keep trying alternate strategies until he finds something that will work. That is when he will begin to taste success.

Quotes from Successful People

- *"Nothing is impossible, the word itself says, 'I'm possible!'"* — **Audrey Hepburn**

- *"I've missed more than 9000 shots in my career. I've lost almost 300 games. 26 times I've been trusted to take the game winning shot and missed. I've failed over and over and over again in my life. And that is why I succeed."* — **Michael Jordan**

- *"It is during our darkest moments that we must focus to see the light."* — **Aristotle Onassis**

- *"Limitations live only in our minds. But if we use our imaginations, our possibilities become limitless."* —**Jamie Paolinetti**

- *"Twenty years from now you will be more disappointed by the things that you didn't do than by the ones you did do, so throw off the bowlines, sail away from safe harbor, catch the trade winds in your sails. Explore, Dream, Discover."* — **Mark Twain**

10 Great Tips

1. Set small goals and reward yourself or your employees when you achieve them.

2. Think about your former achievements and visualize archiving your goals and getting positive results in your mind.

3. Have daily rituals, such as a 25-minute walk and meditation, and take care of yourself mentally and physically.

4. Have a daily short (no more than five things to do) tasks list. Long to-do lists are both frustrating and disappointing.

5. Read inspirational quotes every day and listen to energetic music.

6. Do not stick to only one task for the whole day. Try to spread your energy among different productive activities.

7. Get fifteen minutes of rest and do some stretching after every ninety minutes of work. Eat healthy foods and drink more water.

8. Repeat affirmations and inspirational phrases, such as "I am the best," "I will make it," and "I do not give up."

9. Create a less stressful and happier working environment for yourself and your staff. Split big tasks into smaller activities.

10. Do not be too serious! Having a sense of humor always gives you and others positive energy.

Tools and Resources

1. Book: *Option B: Facing Adversity, Building Resilience, and Finding Joy*, by Sheryl Sandberg, and Adam Grant https://amzn.to/2NGvR9w

2. Book: *The 5 Second Rule: Transform your Life, Work, and Confidence with Everyday Courage*, by Mel Robbins https://amzn.to/2NL1VsT

3. Book: *Captivate: The Science of Succeeding with People*, by Vanessa Van Edwards https://amzn.to/2NIRWEe

4. Book: *The Power of Positive Leadership: How and Why Positive Leaders Transform Teams and Organizations and Change the World*, by Jon Gordon https://amzn.to/2LfldVn

5. Kudos - https://www.kudosnow.com/ - Kudos is an employee recognition system that keeps your workforce motivated, happy, and productive. Give real-time feedback to your employees and get analytic insights into what works best for your business.

How to Manage Your Time Effectively

Why is it Important?

Time flows in only one direction—forward. Nothing you can do will bring yesterday back. Therefore, the limited time you do have must be well accounted for. Many people complain that they are forever running out of time. The problem does not lie with their clocks. It lies with them.

All managers have the same amount of time as Mark Zuckerberg and Bill Gates and Steve Jobs. How were these people able to achieve so much in their lifetime? Besides other capabilities and skills, these people were excellent managers of their time. They were able to prioritize better and use their minutes more effectively. You can learn this too.

Managing your time effectively, reduces stress, and ensures that all tasks are completed as scheduled. It also allows you to set priorities and ensure that important tasks are never overlooked.

Quotes from Successful People

- *"Time is what we want most, but what we use worst."* — **William Penn**

- *"If you want to make good use of your time, you've got to know what's most important and then give it all you've got."* — **Lee Iacocca**

- *"Take care of the minutes and the hours will take care of themselves."* — **Lord Chesterfield**

- *"It's how we spend our time here and now, that really matters. If you are fed up with the way you have come to interact with time, change it."* — **Marcia Wieder**

- *"Never let yesterday use up today."* — **Richard H. Nelson**

10 Great Tips

1. Create task lists and prioritize your activities.

2. Do the most important things first.

3. Learn to say, "No." You should train others to respect your time.

4. Batch similar activities. As an example, if you need to make four phone calls, try to make all of them at a specific time.

5. Turn off notifications from your cell phone and social networks. Try to remove all time wasters.

6. Don't put all tasks back-to-back. Have some buffer time to rest, think, and take care of unpredicted things.

7. Use time management applications to organize your tasks, getting reminders, and reviewing your plans.

8. Learn to delegate un-risky tasks to your employees. Stay away from micromanagement.

9. Review your performance and daily activities.

10. Don't try to do many things at the same time. Multitasking reduces your focus and the quality of your job.

Tools and Resources

1. Rescue Time - https://www.rescuetime.com/ - If you are not sure about how you spend your time online, Rescue Time is an app you can look at. You can define how much time you want to spend on specific websites, and Rescue Time will let you know when that limit is reached.

2. Remember The Milk - https://www.rememberthemilk.com/ - Synch your lists and work to do across all your devices, get timely reminders, and ensure you never forget something important ever again.

3. Focus Booster - https://www.focusboosterapp.com/ - Helps you focus on your tasks, avoid procrastination, and get more work done without increasing stress levels.

4. Asana - https://asana.com/ - Asana helps you manage time and run your business more efficiently so that you have the time to concentrate on the important things.

5. FocusatWill - https://www.focusatwill.com/app/ - Customized for individuals, you get music in the background that is ideally suited to you, helps you stay focused, concentrate on your tasks, and manage your time better than ever before.

How to Make Better Business Decisions

Why is it Important?

Every business decision you make has several short- or long-term outcomes. The products you build, the manufacturing methods you use, the material you select, and the people you hire will all affect your business. Any wrong decision has the potential to put the business back by several years. Some bad decisions may even destroy a business.

There are many causes of a bad decision, such as poor elaboration of alternatives, absence of enough and correct information, improper cost and benefit analysis, and also the mindset of the decision-maker. Decision-making, however, is one of the managerial functions that can be taught and improved by education and practice.

It is also important to remember that no decision is also a decision! Many people tend to put off their decisions, looking for complete information before they take a step. Sometimes this can be a big mistake, so you should be aware of opportunity costs due to the lack of decision-making.

Quotes from Successful People

- *"Wherever you see a successful business, someone once made a courageous decision."* — **Peter Drucker**

- *"The worst business decision you can make is no decision. The needs are not going to go away. Waiting is what's gotten us in the situation we're in now."* — **John Peace**

- *"Decision is the spark that ignites action. Until a decision is made, nothing happens.... Decision is the courageous facing of issues, knowing that if they are not faced, problems will remain forever unanswered."* — **Wilfred A. Peterson**

- *"What's called a difficult decision is a difficult decision because either way you go there are penalties."* — **Elia Kazan**

- *"Stay committed to your decisions, but stay flexible in your approach."* — **Tony Robbins**

10 Great Tips

1. Define your problem or goal precisely. If you do not know what you are going to achieve, you may make wrong decisions and lose your time and other resources.

2. Don't make decisions when you are angry, hungry, or in a hurry. Waiting and thinking a bit is much better than the consequences of wrong decisions.

3. Ask insightful questions to learn more about the matter. Some of these questions are:

    a. What are the important factors in this issue?

    b. How are they related to the issue and each other?

    c. How can I get more advice and information in this regard?

    d. Who are affected by my decision and their opinions about the matter?

4. Collect enough information from reliable sources. Stay away from personal biases.

5. If you are going to make a business decision that affects your employees or other stakeholders, it is highly recommended to involve them in the decision-making process. It has been proven that employees exert more effort and loyalty if you consider them in decision-making.

6. Write down your different options in a table, including the pros and cons of each option based on the important elements that affect the issue.

7. Get advice from professionals, such as your lawyer, your business consultant, or your accountant.

8. Before choosing the best option, try to stay away from overthinking for at least an hour if you can. This approach helps you a lot in making a better decision. You can go for a walk or do some other mindless activities before making your final decision.

9. Review your options again, and make your final decision.

10. Be flexible and revise your decision based on your business situation. Review your business performance regularly to see how effective your decisions are.

Tools and Resources

1. Answer Miner - https://www.answerminer.com - If you don't know how to code and can't make sense of your data, try Answer Miner—designed to work for non-nerds and busy managers.

2. SOFA Statistics - https://www.sofastatistics.com/ - An easy-to-use, open-source statistical program that lets you understand your company data completely and make better business decisions.

3. Book: *Decisive: How to Make Better Choices in Life and Work*, by Chip Heath and Dan Heath https://amzn.to/2LhjW0c

4. Book: *Algorithms to Live By: The Computer Science of Human Decisions*, by Brian Christian, Tom Griffiths https://amzn.to/2ZNyecN

5. Book: *Smart Choices: A Practical Guide to Making Better Decisions*, by John S. Hammond, Ralph L. Keeney, Howard Raiffa https://amzn.to/2HFeTVj

How to Successfully Negotiate

Why is it Important?

Every business needs to deal with people—suppliers, government officials, subcontractors, customers, and employees. Every time you deal with people, you may need to negotiate between different courses of action and the possible choices. Where possible, managers must look for workable, win-win solutions.

Managers who are good at negotiating add significant value to their businesses because of the negotiation process which

- Clarifies expectations of all parties and eventually helps build better business relationships.

- Finds better solutions for problems by understanding the compulsions and requirements of all parties to the discussion.

- Creates clearly defined methods of interaction and works to help minimize future conflict.

Do not be under the impression that every negotiation must result in every demand being met. It is not possible that you get everything you want, and the other party compromises with you on every issue. There will have to be some give-and-take in all situations. Courteous and helpful negotiation ensures that the parties to the negotiation leave satisfied that they have found the best possible solution under the given circumstances and are willing to continue working with each other again.

Quotes from Successful People

- *"The most difficult thing in any negotiation, almost, is making sure that you strip it of the emotion and deal with the facts."* — **Howard Baker**

- *"If you come to a negotiation table saying you have the final truth, that you know nothing but the truth and that is final, you will get nothing."* — **Harri Holkeri**

- *"Diplomacy is the art of letting someone else have your way."* — **Sir David Frost**

- *"It's a well-known proposition that you know who's going to win a negotiation; it's he who pauses the longest."* — **Robert Court**

- *"Never forget the power of silence, that massively disconcerting pause which goes on and on and may last induce an opponent to babble and backtrack nervously."* — **Lance Morrow**

10 Great Tips

1. Be prepared! Learn about your needs, strengths, weaknesses, and also the other party's needs and strengths and weaknesses.

2. Think of a long-term relationship. Do not try to make a deal but lose bigger opportunities later.

3. Listen more than talking. Ask effective questions (How?, When?, Why?) to learn more about the other side's needs and priorities and reasons. Check out their data and claims.

4. Knowing your BATNA (Best Alternative To Negotiated Agreement) is critical to your negotiation. This is the option you have left if you are unable to reach a negotiated agreement.

5. If you have a viable BATNA, you can afford to take tougher stances, but if you do not have a decent BATNA, you had better ensure that the negotiations are fruitful.

6. Start by looking for common points. The two most common techniques of negotiations are cherry-picking and salami slicing:

   a. In cherry-picking, you break down your opponent's arguments or data into smaller parts. You discuss points that are favorable to you and try to disregard the rest.

   b. Salami slicing relates to making several small, apparently insignificant concessions. Your opponent will not feel that much is being given away, but the overall effect brings you closer to your goal.

7. Learn to say, "No." Be firm, fair, and friendly.

8. Do not be in a hurry and look nervous. Watch the party's body language as well.

9. Show the other party that you care about their concerns. Look for a win-win situation.

10. Differentiate between when you need a trained negotiator and when you can handle it yourself. It is always helpful to get some advice if the deal is important for you.

Tools and Resources

1. Book: *Never Split the Difference: Negotiating As If Your Life Depended On It*, by Chris Voss, Tahl Raz https://amzn.to/2zLpM3i

2. Book: *99 Negotiating Strategies: Tips, Tactics & Techniques Used by Wall Street's Toughest Dealmakers*, by David Rosen https://amzn.to/2ZEq9qY

3. Book: *Difficult Conversations: How to Discuss What Matters Most*, by Douglas Stone, Bruce Patton, Sheila Heen https://amzn.to/2NKa4xz

4. Book: *Crucial Conversations Tools for Talking When Stakes Are High, Second Edition*, by Kerry Patterson, Joseph Grenny, Ron McMillan, Al Switzler https://amzn.to/2Lhj9wg

5. Book: *Getting to Yes: Negotiating Agreement Without Giving In*, by Roger Fisher, William L. Ury, Bruce Patton https://amzn.to/2MOB3sk

How to Ask Insightful Questions

Why is it Important?

Every manager or business owner may face situations where employees approach them for guidance and advice regarding a problem. Very often, a busy manager may provide an immediate response without considering all relating factors. By asking insightful questions, the manager can help the employee grow and develop a better understanding of the underlying problem. Asking questions is also important when the level of uncertainty is high. In this regard, solving a complicated problem can be done not by providing an answer immediately but by asking proper questions and considering different scenarios before making a decision.

Insightful questions do not have a cut-and-dried, yes, or no response. They encourage the person to think and consider different alternatives. Managers can use the opportunity to create greater clarity about the problem and challenge people to rethink the basic assumptions they came with.

Insightful questions ask people to examine alternative methods to solve a problem. They also make a person take ownership of the issues and the solution they are offering. The end result is an empowered employee and a more successful business.

Quotes from Successful People

- *"The art and science of asking questions is the source of all knowledge."* — **Thomas Berger**

- *"Curiosity is the process of asking questions, genuine questions, that are not leading to an ask for something in return."* — **Brian Grazer**

- *"I don't like to boss people around. I don't get motivated by telling people what to do, I don't take any pleasure in it. So I manage with curiosity, by asking questions."* — **Brian Grazer**

- *"In my own experience as a C.E.O., I would find myself laying awake at 3 A.M. asking questions about my business, and there weren't management books out there that could help me."* — **Ben Horowitz**

- *"I love the early process of asking questions about a story and deciding which questions matter most."* — **Diane Sawyer**

10 Great Tips

1. Unfortunately, most people try to get answers without having a clear idea of their problems; that's why they target wrong problems, lose a lot of resources, and do not find correct

answers at the end. That shows the importance of asking questions not only to solve our problems but also to be more successful in our businesses or professions.

2. It is important to know that asking questions is not effective until we ask the right questions. Powerful questions encourage people to find answers, improve thinking, and increase participation among team members.

3. Asking questions is so important, especially when the level of uncertainty is high. The following are three main questions that can be so helpful in the problem-solving process:

    a. Who knows about the problem?

    b. Who cares about the problem?

    c. Who can do anything to solve the problem?

4. Ask questions if you want to listen and respond carefully. Most people only think about their next questions or responses without listening precisely to what the responder is saying.

5. Ask open-ended questions that start with why, how, where, when, and what. Do not ask questions that just look for "Yes" or "No" if you try to solve an issue.

6. Don't try to get specific answers by asking questions. Don't ask manipulative questions.

7. The way you ask questions determines the answer you may get. Don't ask negative and blaming questions.

8. Don't ask many questions at the same time. Give the respondent some time to find the correct answer for each question.

9. Analyze and validate your assumptions before asking questions. Remove personal biases from your assumptions and the facts.

10. Keep in mind that creating an environment to ask questions and to be asked by others has a significant role in your business success.

Tools and Resources

1. Book: *Leading with Questions: How Leaders Find the Right Solutions by Knowing What to Ask*, by Michael J. Marquardt
   https://amzn.to/2HHgEB4

2. Book: *Good Leaders Ask Great Questions: Your Foundation for Successful Leadership*, by John C. Maxwell
   https://amzn.to/2ZJrWer

3. Book: *Humble Inquiry: The Gentle Art of Asking Instead of Telling*, by Edgar H. Schein https://amzn.to/2ZKyJEL

4. Book: *The Art of Asking: Ask Better Questions, Get Better Answers*, by Terry J. Fadem https://amzn.to/2NMCY0e

5. Book: *Power Questions: Build Relationships, Win New Business, and Influence Others*, by Andrew Sobel and Jerold Panas
   https://amzn.to/2MRaN0c

How to Define a Workplace Problem

Why is it Important?

Unless you have taken pains to understand a problem correctly, you could be spending all your time working extremely hard on the wrong subject. This will waste your time and effort and will not solve the underlying problem.

A well-defined problem helps you find the right solution because once the underlying issue is correctly defined, it becomes easy to see what needs to be done. Unfortunately, this is not a skill that is taught in most business schools. In many cases, managers have to learn this on their own as they go along.

In many cases, the problem that is immediately visible has nothing to do with the root cause. This may only be the symptom of a more serious issue. Even if you were to solve this problem, the situation would not improve significantly because the underlying issue will remain. Therefore, it is important to explain the problem in-depth and define it in the simplest way possible

Only when the fundamental problem is completely defined and understood can managers get down to resolving the irritant and fixing the issue so that it does not occur again. That is why it is essential to define your business problem correctly.

Quotes from Successful People

- *"If I had an hour to solve a problem, I'd spend 55 minutes thinking about the problem and 5 minutes thinking about solutions."* — **Albert Einstein**

- *"The formulation of the problem is often more essential than its solution, which may be merely a matter of mathematical or experimental skill."* — **Albert Einstein**

- *"A problem well put is half solved."* — **John Dewey**

- *"Creative people are both problem finders and problem solvers."* — **Pearl Zhu**

- *"For an objective approach to a problem, you need to have an overview rather than involvement."* — **Haresh Sippy**

10 Great Tips

1. Problem definition is one of the primary elements of the problem-solving process. By identifying and defining the right problems, we will be able to find and implement effective solutions.

2. One of the first steps in problem definition is to learn about all related people's concerns. As an example, if your business profit is going down, it is recommended to talk to your customers, your marketing employees, and operation staff besides analyzing your competitors and industry trends to have a complete view of the problem.

3. Ask insightful questions to learn about all aspects of the issue. The following are three main questions that can be so helpful in helping you define the problem:

   a. Who knows about the problem?

   b. Who cares about the problem?

   c. Who can do anything to solve the problem?

4. Different people may have various definitions of the same problem, and sometimes they may even manipulate the problem definition for their own benefit. That's why, as a leader, your role is crucial to find out about all aspects of a problem before going for a solution.

5. Consider both internal factors, such as your working process and employees, and also external matters, such as events and competitions, while you are reviewing your problem.

6. One of the best techniques to evaluate people's definitions of the problem is to divide their arguments into three sections:

   a. Individuals' opinions about a specific problem, which is called the claim.

   b. Provided information to support the claim.

   c. The way that claims and provided information are connected. This connection may depend on individuals' emotions, backgrounds, objectives, and biases.

7. Get all the required information, make the conclusion, and write the problem statement.

8. You should take advantage of some tools, such as drawing a rich picture or fishbone diagram, to review the problem and its causes.

9. Write down all the requirements to solve the problem. This can also show you if you have defined the problem correctly.

10. Review the problem definition in different stages of the problem-solving process and revise it if necessary.

Tools and Resources

1. Creating Minds - http://creatingminds.org/tools - Here is a list of some very fundamental tools that you can use to define your workplace problems and find solutions.

2. Book: *The Moment You Can't Ignore: When Big Trouble Leads to a Great Future,* by Malachi O'Connor and Barry Dornfeld https://amzn.to/2Le6iec

3. Book: *How to Measure Anything: Finding the Value of Intangibles in Business,* by Douglas W. Hubbard https://amzn.to/2ZL6IwK

4. Book: *Think Smarter: Critical Thinking to Improve Problem-Solving and Decision-Making Skills,* by Michael Kallet https://amzn.to/2Lhf6Ab

5. Book: *Critical Thinking: A Beginner's Guide to Critical Thinking, Better Decision Making and Problem Solving,* by Jennifer Wilson https://amzn.to/2zOFjzf

How to Validate an Argument

Why is it Important?

In many business situations, there will be many different points of view. Very often, these will develop into arguments, and every party will take a strong position on the subject, leading to an impasse. How will you resolve such a situation in a way that is conducive to the overall growth of the business?

In many cases of business conflict, the participants try to invalidate the argument of the other party. They try to prove that the other party is wrong and that their arguments are weak and worthless.

An alternative method lies in validating the argument. Take the time to see the problem from the other person's perspective. The other person may have a valid point of view that you must consider. It will become easy to do this if you think that examining different points of view will give you deeper insights into a problem and if you think that the argument is adding value by giving you another perspective to the problem being discussed.

Constructive language helps enormously in this situation. How are you so sure that the view you hold is the only correct approach to a problem? Put yourself in the other person's shoes and focus on the real issue. This will help you get to a solution that solves the fundamental problem.

Quotes from Successful People

- *"For good ideas and true innovation, you need human interaction, conflict, argument, debate."* — **Margaret Heffernan**

- *"The aim of argument, or of discussion, should not be victory, but progress."* — **Joseph Joubert**

- *"Argument is meant to reveal the truth, not to create it."* — **Edward de Bono**

- *"Where all is but dream, reasoning and arguments are of no use, truth and knowledge nothing."* — **John Locke**

- *"Convincing yourself doesn't win an argument."* — **Robert Half**

10 Great Tips

1. As a business owner or manager, you may face people who claim many things. The ability to locate and analyze arguments is one of the main aspects of critical thinking that helps you find what is true from false arguments.

2. Through critical thinking, we not only review the form of the argument, which means the relationship between discussions and the conclusion, but we also analyze the practicality of that argument in the real world.

3. To validate an argument, you first need to find an individual's view on the specific issue, which is called the claim.

4. Then review and verify the provided information that has been brought to support the claim.

5. The next step is checking how the claim and provided information are connected.

6. You should also pay close attention to the individual's background, emotions, and objectives when you try to validate his/her arguments.

7. Stay away from your personal biases when you try to verify an argument.

8. Ask insightful questions, such as Why?, Where?, and How? to get more information before making the conclusion.

9. Consult with experts and related people to make sure you have covered all important matters.

10. Never make a decision or judge an argument if you are in a hurry, angry, or hungry.

Tools and Resources

1. Book: *A Rulebook for Arguments*, by Anthony Weston
   https://amzn.to/2ZKUGUa

2. Book: *The Fallacy Detective: Thirty-Eight Lessons on How to Recognize Bad Reasoning*, by Nathaniel Bluedorn and Hans Bluedorn https://amzn.to/2LgeYkp

3. Book: *The Tools of Argument: How the Best Lawyers Think, Argue, and Win*, by Joel P. Trachtman https://amzn.to/2UokBQf

4. Book: *How To Validate Your Startup Business Idea: Simple Self Help Tips That Can Help Startups, Entrepreneurs & Small Business Owners To Validate Their Startup Business Idea*, by Ravi Kikan
   https://amzn.to/2UnWAc8

5. Book: *A Workbook for Arguments, Second Edition: A Complete Course in Critical Thinking*, by David R. Morrow and Anthony Weston https://amzn.to/2MSY3Gn

How to Choose the Right Suppliers

Why is it Important?

The days when businesses made every component of their products by themselves are long gone. Even such a product-obsessed company as Apple is getting its iPhone components made halfway across the world in China, Taiwan, and Korea. Dell gets its computer components sourced from different countries and delivered straight to the customer. Global supply chains have made it possible to increase efficiencies by working in close coordination with suppliers and subassembly part producers.

While this kind of manufacturing activity can be extremely efficient and agile—allowing for fast prototyping and rapid product change—it becomes critical to work with the right suppliers. It has become very easy to find large numbers of suppliers who will offer you competitive pricing and promise great quality. In many cases, however, you may never meet the supplier face-to-face or be able to inspect his facility. Supplier selection becomes critical in such a situation.

Fortunately, global marketplaces have emerged where suppliers can bid for your business and where you can see how other clients have rated them in the past. If your chosen supplier has great client reviews and remarks, chances are you can trust them with your business.

It is wise to start small with a new supplier and increase volumes as you gain confidence. See if you can split your business into two supply chains so that you are not dependent on just one manufacturer. Even with the best supplier, there could be a force majeure situation, such as a fire or an earthquake, that could disrupt supplies.

Quotes from Successful People

- *"A smart manager will establish a culture of gratitude. Expand the appreciative attitude to suppliers, vendors, delivery people, and of course, customers."* — **Harvey Mackay**

- *"Suppliers and especially manufacturers have market power because they have information about a product or a service that the customer does not and cannot have, and does not need if he can trust the brand. This explains the profitability of brands."* — **Peter Drucker**

- *"Our long-standing philosophy that our diverse suppliers must provide high-quality goods and services at competitive prices adds great value to our business."* — **Debra L. Reed**

- *"Big companies often use their leverage to take stakes in would-be suppliers, especially in the technology business."* — **Alex Berenson**

- *"GM is a highly collaborative organization; we rely on a whole tier of suppliers for everything that we do."* — **Tony Scott**

10 Great Tips

1. Determine your needs. You should evaluate your business needs and industry trends to determine what you need from your suppliers.

2. Create a list of the criteria that are important in choosing a supplier. These factors may include:

    a. Price

    b. Quality

    c. Delivery time

    d. Payment time

    e. Customer service

3. Do online search and also ask your reliable sources to refer good suppliers.

4. Compare suppliers based on the factors that are important for you. You can draw a decision-making table, including suppliers' names and their scores based on your criteria.

5. I highly recommend that you talk to current and former customers of the suppliers to get more opinions about them.

6. If possible, visit their manufacturing or production places to learn more about the suppliers.

7. Choose more than one supplier. You should always have backup for your main suppliers.

8. Sign contracts with your suppliers and make sure to include important items, such as price, quality assurance criteria, warranty and return policy, delivery method and time, payment terms and conditions, and also contract termination terms.

9. Try to build a long-term relationship with your suppliers. The quality of your relationship with your supplier has a direct effect on customer satisfaction.

10. Review your suppliers' performance regularly. It is also recommended to check their new pricing, promotions, and products once in a while to see if you can get better deals from them.

Tools and Resources

1. Book: *The Procurement and Supply Manager's Desk Reference*, by Fred Sollish and John Semanik https://amzn.to/2ZKXssE

2. Book: *Supplier Evaluation & Performance Excellence*, by Sherry Gordon https://amzn.to/2L9fP6h

3. Book: *The Vendor Management Office: Unleashing the Power of Strategic Sourcing*, by Stephen Guth https://amzn.to/2L9fZdT

4. Book: *Operations Management For Dummies*, by Mary Ann Anderson, Edward J. Anderson, Geoffrey Parker https://amzn.to/2MIG0Tn

5. Book: *Effective Vendor Management A Complete Guide*, by Gerardus Blokdyk https://amzn.to/2NBSvjk

How to Learn a New Skill

Why is it Important?

There is a basic law of life that if you don't grow, you shrink. Standing still is not an option. Progress will only come to you if you continuously refresh yourself, grow, and develop new skills. Learning new skills also opens up new opportunities for owners of small businesses.

Opportunities in businesses can appear suddenly, and if you do not take advantage of them, your competitors will. That's why it is important to continuously upgrade your skills and stay abreast of what is the latest in your field and related areas. Business owners who do not keep themselves updated will find themselves getting left behind.

It is also important to learn how to handle all aspects of your business even if you will not be handling them yourself all the time. For example, you will often trust your accountant to handle your finances and a lawyer to handle your legal matters. If you learn about account taxes and various laws, however, you will be more qualified to discuss issues with these professionals and will not be in a situation where you are completely dependent on their ideas and advice.

Quotes from Successful People

- *"Every artist was first an amateur."* — **Ralph Waldo Emerson**

- *"Stale water is a poor drink. Stale skill is worse. And the man who walks in his own footsteps only ends where he began."* — **Lloyd Alexander**

- *"Take time learning new skills and principles... Knowledge acquired quickly, flies out the window. In art the tortoise wins."* — **Harley Brown**

- *"One must develop skills that stretch capacities, that make one more than what one is."* — **Mihaly Csikszentmihalyi**

- *"A man is more than the sum of all the things he can do."* — **Bill Clinton**

10 Great Tips

1. Imagine you are a tourist in a city. What would you do? First, you know your goals; you get a map and some ideas about the whole concept.

2. You visit the most famous landmarks, so you should learn about the main elements of the new skill. Do not go into details early.

3. You are not shy to ask questions when you are a tourist. You find reliable sources to answer your questions. You should do the same when you are going to learn a new skill.

4. You take pictures and record videos when you are a tourist and review them later to refresh your great memories. You should take notes and create your own manual when you are learning a new skill. This way, you can review and practice what you learn later. Practice! Practice! Practice!

5. Join learning groups to be in the same environment with other learners and also learn from each other as when you take a tour.

6. Hiring a coach to teach you the new tools and techniques is like hiring a tour guide who shows you the most important things that you may find difficult if you try to do it on your own.

7. Visualize your success and think about what you have learned before going to bed.

8. Focus! Do not try to be a jack-of-all-trades in the shortest period of time.

9. Find an idol. A person who is the best in the skill you want to learn. Watch the videos and read his/her bio to get inspiration and see how to overcome challenges.

10. Do not give up! The first twenty hours that you spend on learning a new skill are so important. If you do not throw in the towel, you will have a big chance to move ahead and be a master in that skill.

Tools and Resources

1. Alison Courses - https://alison.com/ - Select from a large number of courses in a vast range of subjects. There is sure to be a course that applies to your specific domain.

2. Coursera - https://www.coursera.org - Enroll in college-level courses for free. Pay only if you want certification as well.

3. OEDB - https://oedb.org/ - Select from more than 10,000 free online courses to add to your skillset.

4. Udemy - https://www.udemy.com/ - More than 80,000 online courses—many free, some charged—help to build your skills and stay relevant in a fast-changing world.

5. Skillshare - https://www.skillshare.com/ - Skillshare is more focused on soft skills, but these tend to be as important in running a business as knowing the fundamentals of databases and programming.

How to Think Better

Why is it Important?

If you are looking to grow your small business into something more capable and meaningful, the most important tool you have is your mind. It is the mind that invented the wheel, space travel, and everything else in between. It is the quality of your thought process that determines the output you can create.

Is clear and powerful thought restricted to Einstein, Tesla, Jobs, and Gates? Is it possible that everyone develops clear and powerful thought processes? The answer is Yes. If you train yourself, you can think better and develop more powerful insights. Let's see how.

Clear thought can only come to you if you stop focusing on the irrelevant. Every day, you are bombarded with thousands of inputs. Many of these are simply useless, such as the advertisements you see along the road. Others are negative inputs, and they sap your energy. Think of needless arguments and petty jealousies. A few are just thoughts about routine activity, such as the traffic you may meet while driving to the office. But buried in all of these mundane thoughts are a few gems that have the potential to make a major difference in your life and for your business.

Your job is to select the gems and discard what is useless. Do you have the self-discipline to do this?

Quotes from Successful People

- *"Your positive action combined with positive thinking results in success."* — **Shiv Khera**

- *"We cannot solve our problems with the same thinking we used when we created them."* — **Albert Einstein**

- *"Science is a way of thinking much more than it is a body of knowledge."* — **Carl Sagan**

- *"Creative thinking inspires ideas. Ideas inspire change."* — **Barbara Januszkiewicz**

- *"Leadership is a way of thinking, a way of acting and, most importantly, a way of communicating."* — **Simon Sinek**

10 Great Tips

1. Try to remove distractions, such as cell phones and social network notifications, while you are thinking.

2. Reduce fat and alcohol from your diet.

3. Work out regularly.

4. Ask insightful questions (Why?, How?, Where?, When?)

5. Challenge your assumptions. Stay away from personal biases.

6. Learn a new skill and exercise your mind.

7. Do not put too much pressure on yourself. You cannot solve many issues at the same time. Slow down!

8. Meditate and be in the present moment. Don't be upset about the past and worry about the future that may never come.

9. Review the information and sleep on what you think.

10. Don't overthink! Take action and correct your mistakes.

Tools and Resources

1. MindTools - https://www.mindtools.com/ - Use the resources available at MindTools to help you make better business decisions and help your teams to grow.

2. Book: *The Art of Thinking Clearly*, by Rolf Dobelli https://amzn.to/2zAmEal

3. Book: *Thinking Fast & Slow*, by Daniel Kahneman https://amzn.to/2zvdLPw

4. Book: *The 5 Elements of Effective Thinking*, by Edward B. Burger and Michael Starbird https://amzn.to/2zBhICh

5. Book: *Think Smarter: Critical Thinking to Improve Problem-Solving and Decision-Making Skills*, by Michael Kallet https://amzn.to/2MOtKRk

How to Influence People

Why is it Important?

If you have read Malcolm Gladwell's best-selling book *The Tipping Point*, you'll be familiar with "influencers." These are people who have a disproportionate impact on other people and can make people change their opinions and behavior. While many people feel influencers are born that way, there are things you can do to improve your capability to influence people.

An influential businessman is able to merge well with his community and create positive vibes in society. He participates in social activities and has a say in community affairs. As a result, when it comes to local laws and interactions with policymakers and law enforcement agencies, people listen to him and trust him. He can get things done, which has a positive effect on his business.

Influence is all about compelling messaging. You need to have something important to say, and you can put it across in a way that gets people's attention and motivates them to act the way you want them to. Influencers are easy to find in today's age of social media. They stand out by the numbers of people who follow them. Take a look at your social media accounts. Does the number of people you are connected to tell you something?

Quotes from Successful People

- *"The key to successful leadership today is influence, not authority."* — **Ken Blanchard**

- *"Think twice before you speak, because your words and influence will plant the seed of either success or failure in the mind of another."* — **Napoleon Hill**

- *"The greatest ability in business is to get along with others and to influence their actions."* — **John Hancock**

- *"Influence is the new power—if you have influence, you can create a brand."* — **Michelle Phan**

- *"Advertising reflects the mores of society, but it does not influence them."* — **David Ogilvy**

10 Great Tips

1. Influencing is one of the best approaches in changing the behaviors of your employees and customers.

2. Define why you want to influence people and how you are going to measure your success.

3. Focus on a small number of crucial behaviors that will help you achieve your goals. You cannot change people completely, so focus on a couple of vital behaviors that have a direct effect on your business.

4. Encourage people personally to change their behaviors.

5. Engage people in groups so that they can learn from each other.

6. Create an environment in which people are encouraged to change their behaviors.

7. Teach new skills that help people change their behaviors.

8. Use role models and samples to show the benefits of changing their behaviors.

9. Review your performance regularly to see how successful you are in influencing people.

10. Get feedback from them and correct your mistakes.

Tools and Resources

1. Book: *Influence: The Psychology of Persuasion, Revised Edition*, by Robert B. Cialdini https://amzn.to/2HDilQe

2. Book: *Yes!: 50 Scientifically Proven Ways to Be Persuasive*, by Noah J. Goldstein, Ph.D., Steve J. Martin, Robert Cialdini, Ph.D. https://amzn.to/2La5tTz

3. Book: *Influencer: Building Your Personal Brand in the Age of Social Media*, by Brittany Hennessy https://amzn.to/2NIkmP0

4. Book: *Crucial Conversations Tools for Talking When Stakes Are High, Second Edition*, by Kerry Patterson, Joseph Grenny, Ron McMillan, Al Switzler https://amzn.to/2ZBnfHn

5. Book: *Influencer: The New Science of Leading Change, Second Edition*, by Joseph Grenny, Kerry Patterson, David Maxfield, Ron McMillan, Al Switzler https://amzn.to/2L9FlZe

How to Dress Professionally

Why is it Important?

Over the last few years, there have been conflicting views on how people should dress for work. Many companies even encourage their employees to dress casually because they feel that it fosters a friendlier culture and encourages people to be comfortable at work. On the other end of the spectrum are companies where it is (almost) a crime to wear anything other than a business suit.

Employees who are required to interact regularly with clients must be professionally dressed when at work. Clients feel more confident interacting with well-dressed and well-groomed people. While one can argue that "clothes do not make a man," the fact remains that well-dressed employees give out an air of efficiency and confidence.

First impressions matter. When a prospective customer meets you or your employees, he may know little about your business. Will he take a chance on you? It all depends on the feedback other customers give and the impressions you create. Well-dressed, professional employees can generate confidence that shows you and your company are capable organizations that can handle the work being given to you.

Quotes from Successful People

- *"Wearing the correct dress for any occasion is a matter of good manners."* — **Loretta Young**

- *"You've got to have the right attire for the right event. I attend a lot of dinners, a lot of concerts, and I have to be on the red carpet; each has its own dress code, and I have to be prepared. Jeans and a hoodie are great for a concert, but a dinner party?"* — **Amar'e Stoudemire**

- *"Protect your good image from the eyes of negative viewers, who may look at your good appearance with an ugly fiendish eye, and ruin your positive qualities with their chemical infested tongues."* — **Michael Bassey Johnson**

- *"Appearance matters a great deal because you can often tell a lot about people by looking at how they present themselves."* — **Lemony Snicket**

- *"Your appearance, attitude, and confidence define you as a person."* — **Lorii Myers**

10 Great Tips

1. Appearance is so important. Don't ignore the power of self-impression. Your professional appearance also shows your self-confidence.

2. No matter what you wear, it must be clean and ironed.

3. Polish your shoes. Heels should not be too high that you cannot walk properly.

4. Learn in advance about the dress code of the office or the event that you are attending.

5. For women: stay away from tight pants, too much makeup, short skirt, jeans. For men: stay away from casual shirts, tight pants, tight shirts, jeans.

6. Check out your hair, nails, and teeth. They must be clean and look nice.

7. Do not wear too much jewelry or oversized watches.

8. Do not wear strong perfume or cologne. You do not know if other people may have an allergy.

9. Wear professional colors. As an example, a navy suit with a white shirt and a tie for men is a professional set.

10. Do not wear shirts and ties with cartoons and graphics.

Tools and Resources

1. Book: *Dress Like a Man: A Style Guide for Practical Men Wanting to Improve Their Professional Personal Appearance*, by Antonio Centeno, Geoffrey Cubbage https://amzn.to/2NJ1bUT

2. Book: *Effortless Outfits: The Men's Guide to Matching Clothes for Powerful Impression in Personal and Professional Life*, by Robert van Tongeren https://amzn.to/2Lbykas

3. Book: *How to Look Elegant Every Day!: Colors, Makeup, Clothing, Skin & Hair, Posture and More*, by Virginia Lia https://amzn.to/2MN0E4V

4. Book: *How to Get Dressed: A Costume Designer's Secrets for Making Your Clothes Look, Fit, and Feel Amazing*, by Alison Freer https://amzn.to/2HA2thi

5. Book: *How to Look Expensive: A Beauty Editor's Secrets to Getting Gorgeous without Breaking the Bank*, by Andrea Pomerantz Lustig https://amzn.to/2HAW2uq

How to Behave Professionally

Why is it Important?

Regardless of whether you run a small business or a multinational corporation, professional behavior is a must. This professional behavior is not restricted to clients and bosses alone. Everyone must behave professionally all the time.

In professionally run businesses, employees treat each other and clients with courtesy, do not engage in underhanded dealings, and give out the correct information. When managers behave professionally, they set an example of how they want their staff to behave. As a consequence, the overall standard of the workplace will improve.

In successful businesses, clearly set boundaries define expected behavior. Even if there is cause for conflict, it is brought out and discussed without allowing the issue to escalate and becomes serious. Management takes positive actions to improve team bonding and sets in place a friendly and helpful culture.

In a professional organization, people take responsibility for their work. This convinces clients that they are dealing with a mature business with capable management. There is no tendency to do ad hoc work in a professionally run business. Work is well planned, and the schedule is adhered to. This ensures high-quality output.

In the final analysis, behaving professionally will add to your profits and enhance your reputation.

Quotes from Successful People

- *". . . a professional is someone who can do his best work when he doesn't feel like it."* — **Alistair Cooke**

- *"Behavior is a mirror in which everyone displays his own image."* — **Johann Wolfgang von Goethe**

- *"Our names are labels, plainly printed on the bottled essence of our past behavior."* — **Logan Pearsall Smith**

- *"I think professionalism is important, and professionalism means you get paid."* — **Erica Jong**

- *"The true mark of professionalism is the ability to respect everyone else for their styles and always find something positive in every dining experience and highlight it in your thoughts and words."* — **Johnny Iuzzini**

10 Great Tips

1. Be polite! Do not use jargon when you talk in a meeting.

2. Dress professionally.

3. Be in shape and take care of your health.

4. Be a good listener; think before talk.

5. Be punctual.

6. Promise less, deliver more.

7. Don't talk behind others, even your tough competitors.

8. Apologize when you are wrong.

9. Ask proper questions! Be honest in answering questions.

10. Be positive and support others.

Tools and Resources

1. Book: *Cross-Cultural Business Behavior: A Guide for Global Management,* by Richard R. Gesteland https://amzn.to/2zv6oYe

2. Book: *Business Ethics: Decision Making for Personal Integrity & Social Responsibility,* by Laura P. Hartman, Joseph R. DesJardins, Chris MacDonald https://amzn.to/2NI9MY2

3. Book: *Business Ethics: A Stakeholder and Issues Management Approach,* by Joseph W. Weiss https://amzn.to/2ZGV1Ho

4. Book: *The Simple Art of Business Etiquette: How to Rise to the Top by Playing Nice,* by Jeffrey L. Seglin https://amzn.to/2LbLPXs

5. Book: *The Essentials of Business Etiquette: How to Greet, Eat, and Tweet Your Way to Success,* by Barbara Pachter https://amzn.to/2LgJTf1

How to Behave at a Formal Dinner

Why is it Important?

As your company grows, you will find yourself moving upward in your social circle. There will be formal occasions, and there will be occasions when pizza and beer are the norm. It is important to be comfortable in both situations so that you can continue to work on your business even as you build business contacts.

Many people are intimidated when they think of a formal dinner. The sequence in which cutlery is to be used and how the glasses rank in precedence can be pretty difficult to master, but this is a price you pay for success. Once you have mastered the social graces, and these become second nature to you, you can concentrate on the conversation. Otherwise, you would be uncomfortable and would be forever trying to copy the person next to you and would miss out on the opportunities that the dinner offered.

On many occasions, clients judge you by your behavior at a social gathering. They may want to check if you have really "arrived" or are still a pretender in the big leagues. If a businessman has taken the time to learn proper dinner etiquette, it signals that his business is running smoothly and that he has the time (and spare cash) to indulge in the finer things of life.

Quotes from Successful People

- *"Worse than talking with a mouthful, is gossiping with a mouthful!"* — **Anthony Liccione**

- *"The way you treat your food on your plate is a reflection of the way you treat people in your life. Learning how to dine teaches you not just how to eat but how to treat people."* — **Rajiv Talreja**

- *"Consideration is the basis of etiquette, and it starts at home. If you can't show consideration to your spouse, child or family member any*

115

consideration you show outside is shallow and a farce." — **Chinha Raheja**

- *"Sitting down for dinner not only helps you learn, but also teaches you how to listen - which I feel is the most important skill to have. I remember as a kid going around the table listening to everyone's day. It was hard to have the manners not to interrupt back then."* — **Michael Symon**

- *"Simplicity in character, in manners, in style; in all things the supreme excellence is simplicity."* — **Henry Wadsworth Longfellow**

10 Great Tips

1. Learn about different utensils, their placements on the table, and their usage.

2. Don't talk when you are chewing or if you have food in your mouth.

3. You should sit straight as much as you can and not lean over to your food.

4. Except having bread, avoid using your hands or ordering food that needs to be eaten with your hands.

5. Don't use your napkin as a tissue.

6. Say thank you and be courteous with waiters.

7. Put your cell phone on silence, and never check it during dinner.

8. Don't start eating before the host.

9. Don't ask for a to-go box if you have a business dinner in a restaurant.

10. Practice proper dining manners before attending a formal dinner.

Tools and Resources

1. Book: *Modern Manners: Tools to Take You to the Top*, by Dorothea Johnson https://amzn.to/2Pl9vwv

2. Book: *The Essentials of Business Etiquette: How to Greet, Eat, and Tweet Your Way to Success*, by Barbara Pachter https://amzn.to/2ZFAR0z

3. Book: *Business Class: Etiquette Essentials for Success at Work*, by Jacqueline Whitmore https://amzn.to/2ZH4RsS

4. Book: *The Etiquette Advantage in Business, Third Edition: Personal Skills for Professional Success*, by Peter Post, Anna Post, Lizzie Post, Daniel Post Senning https://amzn.to/2ZHG47Q

5. Book: *Essential Manners for Men 2nd Edition: What to Do, When to Do It, and Why*, by Peter Post https://amzn.to/2ZCzzmH

How to Manage a Project Effectively

Why is it Important?

Projects are the lifeline of your business. You could have internal projects (designed to improve your efficiency and processes) or external projects (working with clients). Both are critical to the overall success of your business.

Managing your projects effectively calls for detailed planning and meticulous execution. It requires you to set priorities and distribute resources to various projects. If you put in some effort to take all these actions, you will find that your projects come in on time and do not exceed their planned cost. The result is a better capability, an enhanced reputation, and an overall improved business.

Managing projects effectively also calls for knowing when to say "No." No matter how large your business may be, the time and resources you have at hand will always be limited. You will need to decide which projects to take on immediately, which to defer, and which to refuse. This is the key to ensuring successful business projects.

Quotes from Successful People

- *"Operations keep the lights on, strategy provides the light at the end of the tunnel, but project management is the train engine that moves the organization forward."* — **Joy Gumz**

- *"Running a project without a work breakdown structure is like going to a strange land without a road map."* — **J Phillips**

- *"The P in PM is as much about 'people management' as it is about 'project management.'"* — **Cornelius Fichtner**

- *"Being a Project Manager is like being artist, you have the different colored process streams combining into a work of art."* — **Greg Cimmarrusti**

- *"No matter how good the team or how efficient the methodology, if we're not solving the right problem, the project fails."* — **Woody Williams**

10 Great Tips

1. Define the scope of the project. What are you going to achieve? Who is going to approve the project, and what are his expectations? Make sure all stakeholders approve the scope and objectives of the project.

2. Which types of resources in terms of human resources, information, and money do you have?

3. What is the deadline for completing the project?

4. Assemble your team. What skills and personalities do your team members need to have to accomplish the mission?

5. Develop a project plan, including the steps that need to be taken to finish the job, expected timelines, required resources, and job responsibilities. Don't forget to share your plan with your team and other stakeholders before execution.

6. Create milestones and small goals and review your team's progress in achieving them.

7. Develop a risk management plan. What if your plan does not go as you predicted? What if you do not get the required resources on time? What if you face unexpected issues?

8. Have regular meetings with your team. Stay away from micromanagement.

9. Be flexible and change your plan if required.

10. Document all important steps, expenses, and procedures.

Tools and Resources

1. Quire - https://quire.io/ - Explicitly designed for small teams, Quire helps you manage large complex tasks by breaking them down into subtasks that are easier to manage.

2. Basecamp - https://basecamp.com/ - Feature-rich and small business friendly, Basecamp is ideal for managing many different streams of complex activities.

3. Trello - https://trello.com/ - Get your teams collaborating better than ever before and managing projects efficiently using Trello. It has a completely visual GUI that makes project management very intuitive.

4. Asana - https://asana.com/ - An easy-to-use, web-based project management solution, Asana is clean and uncluttered and highly customizable. Ideal for use by small businesses where large objectives need to be broken into smaller milestones and managed individually.

5. Casual - https://casual.pm/ - A completely visual, easy-to-use tool to manage many different projects on a single interface. See what is going on and manage all projects simultaneously.

How to Get More Organized at Work

Why is it Important?

Do you like unpleasant surprises at work or home? No one does, but many people live with them daily and come to work, wondering what else could go wrong. If you want to avoid unpleasant surprises and keep the law, the IRS, clients, and employees on your right side, then it is important to stay organized and manage your work correctly.

Being organized at work ensures that all your activities are planned and synchronized. Your entire business marches to the same drumbeat, and you can plan for and anticipate events well in time. Being organized also ensures that you can manage your resources correctly, and your projects do not need any last-minute quick fixes to work.

Employees feel good about working in a well-organized environment. They can plan their work and will be able to meet any commitments you may require. The personal lives of people working in an organized business are better managed because they can predict their availability more accurately. This leads to a well-run business and happier clients and employees.

Quotes from Successful People

- *"Organizing is what you do before you do something, so that when you do it, it is not all mixed up."* — **A. A. Milne**

- *"A woman with organizing skills can run a construction company without ever picking up a hammer and nail."* — **Warren Farrell**

- *"Eliminate physical clutter. More importantly, eliminate spiritual clutter."* — **D.H. Mondfleur**

- *"For every minute spent organizing, an hour is earned."* — **Benjamin Franklin**

- *"One may walk over the highest mountain one step at a time."* — **John Wanamaker**

10 Great Tips

1. Have daily task lists for your professional matters and a weekly master list for whatever you need to do during the week.

2. Delegate less important tasks to people who can do that for you.

3. Set up a filing system and don't collect all the documents on your desk. Have a clean desk.

4. Reduce distractions, such as social networks, texts, and mobile applications' notifications.

5. Stay away from multitasking and doing different things at the same time.

6. Take breaks and refresh your mind and body.

7. Use technology effectively. There are many online tools and mobile applications that help you get more organized.

8. Organize your computer and remove useless icons and materials from your desktop.

9. Split large tasks into smaller ones.

10. Check out your office every three months and throw away useless documents and materials.

Tools and Resources

1. Trip it https://www.tripit.com - Organize your trips effectively and efficiently with this great app.

2. Unrool.me https://unroll.me/ - Clean your email box and unsubscribe from whatever you do not want easily.

3. Sprout Social - https://sproutsocial.com/ - Keep track of the social media accounts associated with your business. Get rich

reports on how effective your interactions are and whether or not you are successful in reaching your audience.

4. TimeCamp - https://www.timecamp.com - Use TimeCamp to keep track of your projects, manage invoices, and stay organized and in control of all your projects. The user interface is easy to use, and you spend very little time to get used to the solution and improve your efficiency.

5. Forecast - https://www.forecast.app/ - A combined project management and resource management tool that will help you organize your work better and cut down inefficiencies. An ideal tool to ensure seamless collaboration.

How to Track and Manage Your Business Expenses

Why is it Important?

Cash flow is the lifeblood of any business. You could have a great product and a large number of clients, but if your business does not generate positive cash flow, you will be facing bankruptcy very soon. For this reason, it is important to track and manage your business expenses and ensure that more money is coming into the business than is going out.

It is also necessary to understand that start-up companies need investment, and in the early life of your business, you will be putting in more money than you will be taking out. But if you want to build a viable business, you must ensure that you keep close track of what you are spending money on. Many business people make the mistake of spending money on things that are not necessary for their business. For example, do you really need to buy that shiny new truck to make deliveries? Would it not be better to look around for a good secondhand vehicle and use it instead? Such a simple (and practical) decision will free up a large amount of cash that you can use to improve your product and its marketing.

By keeping close track of your expenses, you have a good understanding of how your business is progressing. You can identify activities where you are losing money and where you are making money and can make necessary improvements to your working methods. You can also forecast expenses more accurately. The result is a business that is viable and has a good chance of becoming self-sustaining.

Quotes from Successful People

- *"Beware of little expenses. A small leak will sink a great ship."* — **Benjamin Franklin**

- *"Look everywhere you can to cut a little bit from your expenses. It will all add up to a meaningful sum."* — **Suze Orman**

- *"Balancing your money is the key to having enough."* — **Elizabeth Warren**

- *"Start with the end in mind."* — **Stephen R. Covey**

- *"What's measured improves."* — **Peter F. Drucker**

10 Great Tips

1. If you respond to a sudden cash-flow situation and start a vigorous cost-cutting exercise, you can do more harm than good. It is the steady savings that are most important because they can add up to a lot over a year.

2. Take care of your energy bills. Ensure you start a graph in a spreadsheet (e.g., MS Excel or use software such as QuickBooks, and add an entry for every month's energy bill. This will tell you how you are doing. Show this graph to your employees to make them aware of the costs.

3. Where appropriate, rent instead of owning business premises. Renegotiate your lease every time you get an opportunity.

4. Be careful about saving money in business practices. Don't cut so close that you hurt the business itself. The first rule of

123

thumb in this area is to ensure that money goes out late and comes in on time (if not earlier).

5. Pay your dues on the due date and take pains to ensure that your collections are on time, and the outstanding balances are minimized. You may need to be aggressive on this and call daily to collect if required. Remember that the crying baby gets the milk.

6. Read your contracts carefully. Are you giving your vendors/customers any benefits that are not written in the contract? If so, then you can always note these and get better terms when you negotiate the next contract.

7. Ensure your inventory stays as small as possible without hurting your business. Remember the management maxim that "inventory is a sign of uncertainty." If you can plan your business well (reduce uncertainty), your inventories will come down.

8. So much has changed technologically that you can get enormous benefits if you take the pains to learn. Switch to cloud computing. You do not need to buy that expensive office software and servers when you can switch to a cloud vendor—Google is an example—at a fraction of the cost.

9. What is your core work; where do you add genuine value? Keep that in-house and consider outsourcing everything else to specialist firms. If you are a financial advisor, your core is analysis and advice. Everything else (including accounting and billing) is support. Keep a core group and outsource everything else.

10. Review your business expenses twice a year and see how you can reduce them.

Tools and Resources

1. Xero - https://www.xero.com/us/ - Built specifically for small businesses, Xero has all the features you need. You can even convert Xero files to be compatible with full-fledged

accounting solutions, such as QuickBooks, to cater to business expansion.

2. PlanGuru - https://www.planguru.com/ - A perfect solution for the budgeting, planning, and forecasting needs of small businesses. Import financial data from MS Excel or any other accounting solution.

3. FreshBooks - https://www.freshbooks.com/ - Cash flow is the lifeblood of any business. With FreshBooks, you ensure that your billing stays up to date and your business prospers.

4. InDinero - https://www.indinero.com/ - A complete accounting and tax handling solution built specifically for small businesses. Keep track of your financials and manage your day-to-day operations efficiently.

5. Expensify - https://www.expensify.com/ - Complete, end-to-end management of your business expenses. Empower your employees to report expenses as they occur and automatically upload them to your accounting systems. Ensure zero lag accounting.

How to Manage Health and Safety at Work

Why is it Important?

No one doubts that building a business environment where employees are healthy and can work safely is crucial. There are many practical reasons for doing so, as well as ensuring workplace safety and healthy working conditions.

Employees appreciate an owner taking the effort (and spending money) to make their work environment safer and healthier. The safety culture you establish permeates to your employees, and you will find them adopting better working practices as well. The net result is fewer working hours lost, fewer insurance claims, a reduction in your legal hassles, and overall cost benefits.

Very often, your customers are impressed when your work is efficient and safe. Imagine a well-run auto garage where everything is in its right place, there are no oil puddles and loose equipment that could hurt workers, and the owner takes care to invest in the right tools and train the staff well. It stands to reason that such a garage will be more efficient, safer, and attract more loyal customers than a dirty sweatshop that just gets the work done.

Quotes from Successful People

- *"Health is the greatest gift, contentment the greatest wealth, faithfulness the best relationship."* — **Buddha**

- *"Early to bed and early to rise makes a man healthy, wealthy and wise."* — **Benjamin Franklin**

- *"To keep the body in good health is a duty... otherwise we shall not be able to keep our mind strong and clear."* — **Buddha**

- *"Time and health are two precious assets that we don't recognize and appreciate until they have been depleted."* — **Denis Waitley**

- *"A healthy outside starts from the inside."* — **Robert Urich**

10 Great Tips

1. Paying attention to workplace health and safety can prevent your business from many potential troubles and lawsuits.

2. Learn about safety laws and regulations based on your business.

3. Find out safety risks and hazards at your workplace.

4. Train your employees regarding health and safety at work.

5. Develop an effective working manual, including safety instructions.

6. Review safety guidelines once a year.

7. Reduce workplace stress.

8. Maintain clean and organized work areas.

9. Ask your staff to report health and safety issues.

10. Have a system to check the air quality of your workplace.

Tools and Resources

1. At Work - https://www.nsc.org/work-safety - Use this comprehensive program to make your workplace safer and minimize workplace injuries.

2. Book: *The Manager's Guide to Workplace Safety*, by R. Scott Stricoff and Donald R. Groover https://amzn.to/2ZwNsmJ

3. Book: *Workplace Safety and Health (Occupational Safety & Health Guide Series)*, by Thomas D. Schneid https://amzn.to/2zszw29

4. Book: *Workplace Safety: A Guide for Small and Midsized Companies*, by Dan Hopwood and Steve Thompson https://amzn.to/2Zhz32v

5. Book: *PeopleWork: The Human Touch in Workplace Safety*, by Kevin Burns https://amzn.to/32aZOTf

How to Sit Correctly Behind your Desk

Why is it Important?

Many of us spend long hours at our desks. You could be typing, reading, or simply talking to many people while you are sitting down. If you pay attention to your posture, you will not only look better and find yourself giving a lot more attention to your work, but you will also experience lesser low back pain and hunched shoulders. People who have a good work posture suffer fewer injuries and can perform better over the long term.

Good posture at your desk also allows your lungs to oxygenate your blood better, which leads to reduced fatigue and better quality of work. You are more alert, and anyone interacting with you will find your personality more impressive. Alert and attentive people send out the message that they are interested in the business and that they can be relied upon to do a good job.

The next time you are at your desk, observe your thought processes when you are erect and alert, and when you are slouching or half sprawling at your desk. You will be able to notice the difference easily.

Quotes from Successful People

- *"Your task is to sit up straight, not to be held straight."* — **Marcus Aurelius**

- *"Good posture can be successfully acquired only when the entire mechanism of the body is under perfect control."* — **Joseph Pilates**

- *"Mere physical sitting is not enough. You have to sit carefully and attentively. Let your body and breathing sit. Let your mind and emotions sit. Let your blood circulation sit. Let everything sit. Then your sitting becomes indestructible, immovable."* — **Taizan Maezumi**

- *"Never slouch, as doing so compresses the lungs, overcrowds other vital organs, rounds the back, and throws you off balance."* — **Joseph H. Pilates**

- *"The quickest way to change your emotional state is to change your body."* — **Tony Robbins**

10 Great Tips

1. Adjust the chair height to have your feet flat on the foot support or the floor and that your knees and hips are aligned.

2. Sit up far back in the chair and straight.

3. It is recommended to recline the back of your chair at almost a 100° angle.

4. Put the keyboard close so that your elbows can make almost 90° angles.

5. Put the monitor directly in front of you a couple of inches above eye level.

6. Your distance to the monitor should be at least your arm's length or 20 inches.

7. Move and raise your shoulders every 30–45 minutes.

8. Go for a short walk after prolonged sitting.

9. Put lower and upper back support on your chair if needed.

10. Buy a good agronomy office chair. Never sacrifice your health to save money!

Tools and Resources

1. Sitting Right - https://www.nhs.uk/ - The UK National Health Service website has some very practical advice for people who work long hours at their desks.

2. Book: *Deskbound: Standing Up to a Sitting World*, by Kelly Starrett https://amzn.to/2KYSBzL

3. Book: *Overcoming Poor Posture: A Systematic Approach to Refining Your Posture for Health and Performance*, by Steven Low and Jarlo Ilano https://amzn.to/2KVTKrD

4. Book: *Pain-Free Posture Handbook: 40 Dynamic Easy Exercises to Look and Feel Your Best*, by Lora Pavilack, Nikki Alstedter, Dr. Elizabeth Wisniewski DC https://amzn.to/327v2KC

5. Book: *Stretching to Stay Young: Simple Workouts to Keep You Flexible, Energized, and Pain Free*, by Jessica Matthews https://amzn.to/2KXxMEP

How to Eat to be Healthier and More Productive

Why is it Important?

Many times we are told, "You are what you eat." Sadly, our culture promotes fast food, cramming something to keep the hunger pangs away and eating out rather than going in for home-cooked meals. The fact is that most fast food and meals in a restaurant are designed to be tasty rather than healthy. This means lots of fat, starch, sugars, and salt. Over the years, this kind of food can ruin your health.

While we may understand that breakfast is the most important meal of the day, many busy people do not take the time to get a healthy, nutritious meal to start the day. As a result, they end up being low on energy and underperforming.

Many people have discovered the value of eating vegetables and fruits. While being vegan or not is a matter of personal choice, it is important to get enough natural fiber into your system to ensure you stay healthy. Healthy food will be more filling, it will take a little longer to digest, and it will smoothen out the rapid peaks and troughs in your blood sugar that can come from eating too much of refined and ready-to-eat meals. The end result of a healthy diet is a healthy individual who can perform true to his/her potential.

Quotes from Successful People

- *"The food you eat can be either the safest and most powerful form of medicine or the slowest form of poison."* — **Ann Wigmore**

- *"Pay the farmer or pay the hospital."* — **Birke Baehr**

- *"You don't have to cook fancy or complicated masterpieces—just good food from fresh ingredients."* — **Julia Child**

- *"Came from a plant, eat it; was made in a plant, don't."* — **Michael Pollan**

- *"Just like keeping a healthy diet is important to maintaining a healthy lifestyle, eating the right foods is just as important for getting the most out of your workout."* — **Marcus Samuelsson**

10 Great Tips

1. First, decide what you are going to have for lunch or during the day in advance. Don't allow your hunger to make decisions for you.

2. Eat small, more frequent portions to keep your glucose at a constant level and increase your productivity.

3. Bring healthy snacks, such as fruits, vegetables, and nuts, to your office.

4. Don't drink too much caffeine.

5. Never skip a healthy breakfast.

6. Drink eight glasses of water per day. You can use some apps to remind you not to forget that.

7. Don't eat heavy meals. It really affects your performance.

8. Reduce the amount of fat and dairy products.

9. Take the required vitamins, especially Vitamin D, which most people don't have enough.

10. Take your blood test at least once a year.

Tools and Resources

1. Book: *Eat Dirt: Why Leaky Gut May Be the Root Cause of Your Health Problems and 5 Surprising Steps to Cure It*, by Dr. Josh Axe
https://amzn.to/325jx6w

2. Book: *Mini Habits for Weight Loss: Stop Dieting. Form New Habits. Change Your Lifestyle Without Suffering*, by Stephen Guise
https://amzn.to/2HoJ6HJ

3. MyFitnessPal - https://www.myfitnesspal.com/ - It all begins with what you eat. Keep track of your calories, food quality,

and activities through this application. Join a large community of fitness conscious people and stay motivated.

4. FatSecret - https://www.fatsecret.com/ - One of the best apps to help you watch what you eat.

5. Sworkit - https://sworkit.com/ - The app name means "simply work it." It has hundreds of exercises and millions, yes, millions of users who have worked their way to fitness. You can select from as little as 5 minutes at a time and get to a fitter, healthier you.

How to Reduce Work Stress

Why is it Important?

While some work pressure and stress are inevitable in any business, you will be far better off over the long term working in a stress-free, low-pressure situation. A stress-free working environment allows you to plan better and execute your plans more effectively.

Employees in a stress-free working environment are more productive and innovative because they have no fear of failure or the consequences of failure. Therefore, if you want to unleash the power of creativity in your employees, work actively to create an environment where stress is minimized, and the fun quotient is high. In such an environment, motivation will always be high, and innovation will increase.

Lower stress levels are also associated with better health—both physical and mental. By promoting a comfortable work environment, you will be able to lead a better life and enjoy better relations with your employees, customers, and associates. In such a workplace, you will find that your employees will put in extra effort to make your business a success.

While it may not be possible to remove all stress and pressure at work, keeping it within healthy and safe limits will definitely help your business.

Quotes from Successful People

- *"Instead of always asking how to get others to approve of you... learn to ask: What do I really want, the applause of the crowds or to quietly have my own life?"* — **Guy Finley**

- *"If you can change your mind, you can change your life."* — **William James**

- *"Much of the stress that people feel doesn't come from having too much to do. It comes from not finishing what they've started."* — **David Allen**

- *"The greatest weapon against stress is our ability to choose one thought over another."* — **William James**

- *"Do not anticipate trouble or worry about what may never happen. Keep in the sunlight."* — **Benjamin Franklin**

10 Great Tips

1. First, you need to find stress triggers. For two weeks, write down the situations that made you stressed.

2. Keep in mind that stress is the meaning we give to different phenomena. Whatever is stressful for us might not be for others, so we need to review our thoughts.

3. Ask yourself the following questions:

    a. How important is the situation?

    b. Will I be worried about this situation if I look at it three years from now?

    c. How can I use this situation to improve myself?

4. Eat healthy, exercise regularly, and sleep well.

5. Take a break at least every ninety minutes and refresh your mind. Do some stretching if you sit a lot behind a desk.

6. Getting organized and learning time management skills can reduce a lot of work stress.

7. Stop overthinking, and do not worry about things that are not under your control.

8. Learn to say NO! Sometimes a proper NO is much more effective than many unreal YESES.

9. Get support and talk to your colleagues about the issues. Keep in mind that you can talk about all professional issues without offending others if you speak politely and respectfully.

10. Be flexible in your decisions. Being too strict without having other options is always stressful.

Tools and Resources

1. Happify - https://www.happify.com/ - Scientific methods to make your employees happy and stress-free.

2. FocusatWill - https://www.focusatwill.com/ - Increase your office productivity by at least 4x by getting hundreds of hours of music tailored to your specific organization.

3. ActiveCollab - https://activecollab.com/ - Use ActiveCollab to improve coordination within your teams and reduce stress levels associated with difficult projects.

4. AgreeDo - https://www.agreedo.com/index.html - Minimize the stress related to completing complex tasks and reduce the effort taken to set up meetings and record the decisions taken.

5. Focus Watch - http://focuswatchapp.com/ - Use Focus Watch along with your Apple devices to ensure your employees plan their work and take breaks optimally, so that workplace stress is minimized.

How to Find the Best Business Travel Deals

Why is it Important?

Even small businesses today can have global exposure. You could be sourcing material from many different places and selling (through e-commerce) to clients far away. In such a business environment, increased and extensive travel is a basic requirement.

If you are spending a fair amount of money on travel expenses, it makes sense to see where you can economize and get the best deals. Even a 10 percent saving in your tickets and hotel bills can make a substantial difference to your bottom line. This saving can be used in marketing and sales to generate additional income. Getting good business deals also allows your employees to be more efficient while traveling. They can meet several clients or associates in a single well-planned trip.

There are many ways to get good business deals and save on travel and related expenses. Many small businesses tie up with hotel chains and airlines to ensure them a minimum number of bookings annually to claim bulk discounts. You can also use modern technology, such as videoconferencing, to reduce the frequency of travel.

Quotes from Successful People

- *"Wherever you go, go with all your heart."* — **Confucius**

- *"The world is a book, and those who do not travel read only a page."* — **Saint Augustine**

- *"The best education I have ever received was through travel."* — **Lisa Ling**

- *"Exploration is really the essence of the human spirit."* — **Frank Borman**

- *"I never travel without my diary. One should always have something sensational to read in the train."* — **Oscar Wilde**

10 Great Tips

1. If you travel a lot, choose a credit card that gives you a lot of points for flights.

2. It is highly recommended to have a perk number from the airlines that you fly with to collect mileage.

3. Ask if you can upgrade your seat for free or a little extra when you check in at the airport.

4. Based on some studies, Tuesdays and Thursdays are the best days to fly in terms of pricing.

5. Check out https://www.google.com/flights/

6. Check out http://www.airfarewatchdog.com/

7. Check out https://www.kayak.com/

8. Check out https://www.expedia.com

9. Check out https://www.priceline.com/

10. It is always recommended to make a phone call besides surfing the Internet to see if you can get a good deal from the airlines.

Tools and Resources

1. Expedia - https://www.expedia.com - One of the best tools to find travel deals.

2. TravelPerk - https://www.travelperk.com/ - Plan trips, book flights, manage expenses, configure travel policies all in one easy-to-use free application.

3. Expensify - http://www.expensify.com/ - Manage the travel expenses of your employees even as they are still traveling. Simply take a photo of a bill and the data automatically gets loaded to the correct expense account.

4. TripIt - https://www.tripit.com/ - Give TripIt a list of authorized email IDs, and it will automatically search their inboxes for travel details and ticket information. Once the details are with TripIt, it checks for flight delays, manages taxi and hotel bookings, and updates individual calendars.

5. Points - https://www.points.com/ - A solution to club all the points you have accumulated and use them gainfully. You can even swap your points with others and buy more miles.

How to Stay Healthy During Long-Haul Flights

Why is it Important?

Let's face it. When you go on that long-haul flight for business work, you do not have the luxury of taking two days off to recover from the time zone changes, jet lag, and fatigue. You are expected to be productive and get to work soon after you land.

There are many factors that go against your health on a long-haul flight. To begin with, you are locked up in a cramped room with several hundred others all breathing the same air. The pressure in the airplane is lower than at ground level, which means you have less oxygen to work with. Humidity is low, and this can lead to drying up of your respiratory system, leading to discomfort. Sitting in a small seat for long hours can give you cramps and lead to blood clots forming in your veins. This can be fatal.

You need to take charge of your health on a long-haul flight. Drink a lot of water, walk up and down the aisles, eat lightly, and take short naps. This will ensure you get off in the best possible condition after a long flight.

Quotes from Successful People

- *"A healthy attitude is contagious but don't wait to catch it from others. Be a carrier."* — **Tom Stoppard**

- *"Good food is healthy food. Food is supposed to sustain you so you can live better, not so you can eat more. Some people eat to live, and some people live to eat."* — **Yolanda Adams**

- *"As much as you can eat healthy, it's also important to remember to drink healthy too. Tea is very healing."* — **Kristin Chenoweth**

- *"Everyone has their own definition of a healthy lifestyle, and mine has come to mean making health a priority but not an obsession."* — **Daphne Oz**

- *"A long healthy life is no accident. It begins with good genes, but it also depends on good habits."* — **Dan Buettner**

10 Great Tips

1. Don't eat too much. Proper digestion is less during flights, so it is better not to be full.

2. Avoid or consume only a very low amount of caffeine or alcohol.

3. Always take some snacks, such as a protein bar, nuts, or a banana, with you.

4. Take a neck pillow and an eye mask to help you sleep better.

5. Download and listen to mediation songs and relaxing music during your flight.

6. Drink a lot of water.

7. Move, go for a short walk, and stretch your body at least every two hours.

8. Dress comfortably. Your dress is better to have layers so that you can take it off or add it based on the temperature inside the plane.

9. It is always recommended to take an aisle seat since it makes it much easier for you to go to the bathroom or stretch your body during the flight.

10. Always ask during checking in to see if you can upgrade your seat for free or by paying a little more. You never know; sometimes, airlines have empty seats and can do it for you.

Tools and Resources

1. Smarter Travel - https://www.smartertravel.com/ - Learn great travel tips. Follow these simple tips to stay as healthy and comfortable as you possibly can.

2. WebMD - https://wb.md/2Ail6C5 - Learn what yoga and related activities can do to keep you healthy during those long-haul flights.

3. Health Tips - https://www.medicalnewstoday.com/articles/237345.php - A detailed discussion of how to minimize discomfort and stay healthy during long-haul flights. It also has a great section on handling jet lag.

4. Flying Stress - http://www.fearofflyinghelp.com/ - This free online course by a senior pilot from a major airline will help those who find flying stressful.

5. Eating Tips - https://bit.ly/2DQzNQM - What to eat and what to avoid on those long-haul trips. Eat right and arrive in good shape.

How to Overcome Negative Thoughts

Why is it Important?

It is well documented that your thoughts have a very powerful impact on your personality, your health, and your capacity to interact with people around you. All of these will affect the way you run your business and will go a long way in determining whether your business succeeds or fails.

While all of us will face difficulties and problems in life and at work, how we react to our circumstances will determine the final outcome. The nature of our thoughts has a major role in this matter. If your thoughts are negative, you will tend to feel like a victim and think that everyone is against you. Negative people tend to see enemies even though they may not exist. This spoils working relationships. As a result, you may end up worsening your problems with your negative thoughts.

It is possible to overcome negative thoughts, however, but only if you are serious about doing so. Whenever a defeatist or negative thought comes to your mind, recognize what is happening, and do not let it direct your actions. Ask yourself, "What if my thinking is wrong?" "Could it be that I am creating difficulties for myself by my negative thinking?" It is possible to defeat negativity once you recognize it.

Quotes from Successful People

- *"Once you replace negative thoughts with positive ones, you'll start having positive results."* — **Willie Nelson**

- *"Negative thoughts stick around because we believe them, not because we want them or choose them."* — **Andrew J. Bernstein**

- *"When the negative thoughts come—and they will; they come to all of us - it's not enough to just not dwell on it... You've got to replace it with a positive thought."* — **Joel Osteen**

- *"Be a force of love as often as you can and turn away negative thoughts whenever you feel them surface."* — **Wayne Dyer**

- *"Your thoughts carry you wherever you want to go. Weak thoughts don't have the energy to carry you far!"* — **Israelmore Ayivor**

10 Great Tips

1. Whenever you have negative thoughts, ask yourself if this thought is true, important, or helpful.

2. Don't try to stop thinking! Allow thoughts to come and go.

3. Tell yourself that these thoughts are not the real me. These are just some thoughts that come and go naturally.

4. Try to distract your mind to something positive. As an example, think about the achievements that you have had in your life at different ages.

5. Try to have positive people around you.

6. Write down negative thoughts on a piece of paper and then throw it in the trash.

7. Change your environment.

8. Keep in mind that there are two types of problems: 1) those that are under your control so you can always find solutions for them and 2) those that are not under your control so you should not worry about them. That's life!

9. Meditate even for five minutes.

10. Work out! That's the best way to remove negativity from your mind.

Tools and Resources

1. Book: *Negative Self-Talk and How to Change It*, by Shad Helmstetter Ph.D. https://amzn.to/2ZtOUpR

2. Book: *365 Days of Positive Self-Talk*, by Shad Helmstetter Ph.D. https://amzn.to/32aUb7z

3. Book: *A Year of Positive Thinking: Daily Inspiration, Wisdom, and Courage*, by Cyndie Spiegel https://amzn.to/2HrJXrb

4. Gratitude - http://getgratitude.co/ - Spend just a few minutes on this app and rewire your brain for positivity.

5. Headspace - https://apple.co/2DFNC3F - An extremely popular app that has helped hundreds of thousands of people overcome stress, negativity, and emotional turmoil.

How to Start Your Day to be Happier and More Productive

Why is it Important?

Being happy and cheerful brings positive energy to work and creates an environment where people look to cooperate and collaborate. This increases the collective output of the group. It is very easy to notice the difference between happy and unhappy places of work. If you start your workday by being happy and cheerful, you will find that you and your staff will be more productive.

Even if you have problems at work (and who doesn't?), you will find better solutions if your staff cooperates with each other and works as a team in a happy environment. Many businesses start the workday with a small meditation session where everyone gets together to spend a few peaceful moments. This reduces the stress people may have carried from home and improves team spirit. People realize the value of being together as a team and begin helping each other rather than only caring about their own backs. If your team can adapt such a culture, your business will prosper.

Quotes from Successful People

- *"Amateurs sit and wait for inspiration, the rest of us just get up and go to work."* — **Stephen King**

- *"It is not enough to be busy... The question is: what are we busy about?"* — **Henry David Thoreau**

- *"Efficiency is doing better what is already being done."* — **Peter Drucker**

- *"Productivity is never an accident. It is always the result of a commitment to excellence, intelligent planning, and focused effort."* — **Paul J. Meyer**

- *"Cell phones, mobile e-mail, and all the other cool and slick gadgets can cause massive losses in our creative output and overall productivity."* — **Robin S. Sharma**

10 Great Tips

1. Don't check your emails and social media when you wake up.

2. Start your day with a mild workout. Don't start your day with heavy exercise.

3. Meditate after you wake up.

4. Practice gratitude and count your blessings.

5. Drink a glass of warm water with some lemon juice before having your breakfast.

6. Never skip a good breakfast.

7. Work on your daily task list.

8. Read the latest news regarding your business or profession.

9. Read inspirational quotes.

10. Listen to energetic music.

Tools and Resources

1. Positive Thinking - http://positivethinking.net/ - Get messages to reinforce positive thinking and change your outlook on life. Proven to work wonders.

2. Realifex - http://www.realifex.com/ - Work with a real life coach and change yourself to a more productive and happy person.

3. Smiling Mind - https://www.smilingmind.com.au/ - This free app has been downloaded by more than three million

people who testify to its value and how it has helped them lead happier, more productive lives.

4. Book: *The Happiness Project: Or, Why I Spent a Year Trying to Sing in the Morning, Clean My Closets, Fight Right, Read Aristotle, and Generally Have More Fun,* by Gretchen Rubin
   https://amzn.to/2KXxTQX

5. Book: *Outer Order, Inner Calm: Declutter and Organize to Make More Room for Happiness,* by Gretchen Rubin
   https://amzn.to/2Zt0HVd

How to Build a Good Habit

Why is it Important?

A habit is something you begin to do subconsciously and automatically without thinking a great deal about it. Once you form a habit, it is very difficult to break it and establish a different behavior pattern. Businesses that understand this matter take great care to form correct habits in their employees, managers, and even their work processes.

Since habits become automatic over time, a good habit is a great way of establishing the right culture in your organization. Take, for example, ethical behavior. If your employees know that under any circumstances you want them only to do the ethical and legal thing, then this is what they will do. Over time, this will become the standard practice of running your business, and you will get a great reputation in the marketplace.

Good habits avoid a lot of trouble for you over the long term. If you have established habits of honesty, punctuality, accuracy in accounting, and ethical behavior, you will prevent a lot of unnecessary trouble in the future. Your business will acquire a reputation to be proud of, and your employees will be looking forward to their day at work. Set up good habits from your first day at work and watch the magic unfold.

Quotes from Successful People

- *"We are what we repeatedly do. Excellence then, is not an act, but a habit."* — **Aristotle**

- *"Winning is a habit. Unfortunately, so is losing."* — **Vince Lombardi**

- *"I never could have done what I have done without the habits of punctuality, order, and diligence, without the determination to concentrate myself on one subject at a time."* — **Charles Dickens**

- *"Thoughts lead on to purposes; purposes go forth in action; actions form habits; habits decide character; and character fixes our destiny."* — **Tryon Edwards**

- *"Habits change into character."* — **Publius Ovidius Naso Ovid**

10 Great Tips

1. Be specific about what you want to achieve. Setting goals always inspires and gives direction.

2. Keep in mind that if you develop a great effective habit, it may create other good habits automatically. As an example, if you try to wake up a little earlier every day and write your to-do list, it may help you be more successful in time management during the day as well.

3. Visualize your success. Imagine you have developed your new habit and its effects in your life.

4. Start small and allow good things to compound in your life! You cannot change everything in a very short period of time.

5. Determine how you can overcome obstacles and distractions. Ask effective questions, such as Why do I need to achieve my goal? Why does this obstacle exist? How can I stick to my plan?

6. Learn to say "No" to distractions.

7. Repeat solid affirmations "I will make it"; "I can do it"; "Nothing can stop me"; "I do not give up."

8. Add your new actions to your to-do lists. You must keep seeing and repeating your new rituals.

9. Be consistent, but not too strict on yourself. Don't be disappointed if you cannot make it the way you planned. It takes time to get rid of an old habit and make a new one.

10. Review your progress and reward yourself.

Tools and Resources

1. Momentum - https://apple.co/2zULCit - Learn what makes you tick and keep close track of your habits and routines. Export data to MS Excel for more detailed analysis.

2. Habitica - https://bit.ly/1HXweoU - This app in a video game format (available for both Android and iOS platforms) tracks your habits and helps you reinforce good habits and correct the bad ones.

3. Book: *Atomic Habits: An Easy & Proven Way to Build Good Habits & Break Bad Ones*, by James Clear https://amzn.to/2ZtxwkZ

4. Book: *The Power of Habit: Why We Do What We Do in Life and Business*, by Charles Duhigg https://amzn.to/2Htj4TR

5. Book: *Hack Your Habits: An Unusual Guide to Escape Motivational Traps, Bypass Willpower Problems and Accelerate Your Success*, by Joanna Jast https://amzn.to/2ZpMXKR

Human Resource Management

How to Hire an Effective Employee

Why is it important?

Your employees are an essential resource with which you conduct your business. They convert your dreams and vision into reality, interact with customers, and carry out the day-to-day operations that are so important to your business. Ask any businessman and he will tell you that getting and retaining a good employee is most important for the growth of the business.

An effective employee adds value to your business. Such employees will produce output beyond what you ask of them. They will go out of their way to keep your business growing and prospering. Such an employee also proves to be a role model for other employees. They will see their devotion to work and be similarly influenced.

You can do much to ensure you get good employees. If you have a reputation for being an ethical employer who pays employees well and provides good working conditions, you will find good people more willing to work for you. It is also important that you give your best employees challenging work that allows them to grow intellectually. Employees are your best asset, and the sooner you realize this, the better for your business.

Quotes from Successful People

- *"If you pick the right people and give them the opportunity to spread their wings and put compensation as a carrier behind it, you almost don't have to manage them."* — **Jack Welch**

- *"I hire people brighter than me and I get out of their way."* — **Lee Iacocca**

147

- *"The competition to hire the best will increase in the years ahead. Companies that give extra flexibility to their employees will have the edge in this area."* — **Bill Gates**

- *"The secret of my success is that we have gone to exceptional lengths to hire the best people in the world."* — **Steve Jobs**

- *"Great vision without great people is irrelevant."* — **Jim Collins**

10 Great Tips

1. Timing your hiring actions: Ensure you have the resources— more so if you are creating a new job. There are many hidden and visible expenses before an employee becomes productive. Be aware of your seasonal needs.

2. Determine your needs: Tabulate and prioritize your requirements. Identify the responsibilities and the skills required. If needed, break up complex jobs into two.

3. Defining the job: Create a detailed job description. Ensure you leave scope for additional duties in the job description. Work out the salary package and the other tangible/intangible benefits you will be offering the individual.

4. Writing job ads: Write a conversational advertisement—do not make the advertisement too complex or stiff. Describe benefits and career advancement opportunities.

5. Posting a job: Post the position on job-related websites and your company's website. Ask your employees to publicize the position through their online social media networks.

6. Creating structured application forms: Ensure that your application form makes it easy to assess and compare candidates. If possible, accept forms online with data going directly into a database.

7. Interviewing candidates: Depending on the complexity of the job being offered, you could hold several rounds of interviews. Ask open-ended questions rather than ones that can be answered with a simple "yes" or "no." Be careful of

asking illegal questions, such as sexual orientation, race, creed, color, and religion.

8. Conducting tests and employee reference check: Ensure that the same test is administered to all candidates. Ask for work references. Do not waste your time asking for personal references.

9. Making a job offer: Make any terms and conditions very clear.

10. Thank other applicants: Thank all applicants, especially those you interviewed. Provide a quick thank-you letter and thanks for their time, saying you are going to keep their information on file and that you'll let them know if any new positions become available.

Tools and Resources

1. Breezy HR - https://breezy.hr - Tracking applications and hiring employees is easy when you use this application tracking and candidate management system.

2. Textio - https://textio.com - A writing tool that is specifically focused on job posts. It predicts how prospective candidates will respond to your job postings and prompts you to write better and get quality responses.

3. Connect - https://connect.clearbit.com - Connect from Clearbit gives you near immediate access to almost anyone's email, location, and personal information. This is a great tool for background research on prospective employees.

4. Calendly - https://calendly.com - Makes it easy for candidates and interviewers to set up meetings at mutual convenience and to create alerts and follow up workflow.

5. MixMax - https://mixmax.com - Gives you complete control over your emails and gives you statistics, such as when seen, downloads, and replies, and allows you to schedule emails.

How to Interview a Potential Employee

Why is it Important?

Even if you are hiring for a short term (e.g., to help with the Christmas rush), you must look at every employee as a long-term asset. After all, you will be entrusting an important part of your business to this person and will be spending resources on onboarding and training. Therefore, it is critical to take your hiring process very seriously and select your employees with care.

The interview is an important part of the employee selection process. It allows you to see the candidate and assess the person better. While the prospective employee's CV could have been produced by an expert and made to look good, when you meet the candidate you can judge how the person speaks, conducts themselves, whether the person is confident and knowledgeable, and if the person will be a good fit for your business.

The interview also allows the potential employee to get a good idea of the work that is required and to see if they fit the role you want this person for. This two-way communication ensures that both parties understand each other well and increases the probability that the employee will be a better fit in your organization.

Quotes from Successful People

- *"I'm not an interviewer. I have conversations."* — **Werner Herzog**

- *"When I'm interviewing someone, I want to make sure that he thought enough to take care of himself—to dress appropriately and to groom himself properly."* — **Bill Rancic**

- *"Interviewing someone is very similar to preparing a character, isn't it? You're just asking questions: 'Who is this person? Why did they make that choice? Why are they doing that?' You're being Sherlock Holmes."* — **Felicity Jones**

- *"One important key to success is self-confidence. An important key to self-confidence is preparation."* — **Arthur Ashe**

- *"A good interviewer is able to ferret out what the applicant is really passionate about. Ask them what they do for fun, what they're reading, try and find out if they have a life outside of work."* — **Nolan Bushnell**

10 Great Tips

1. Arrange the interview room well. Set your candidate at ease by providing a quiet place without any distractions and uncomfortable seating.

2. It is important to break the ice and set a friendly tone for the interview. Introduce yourself and any other members of the interviewing team and explain your function in the organization.

3. As part of the preparation for the interview, have a list of questions you will be asking every candidate and separate lists of questions for candidates to clarify points from the applications or to test their understanding of particular issues.

4. If you are well prepared, the questions will be relevant to the resume, fill in gaps, and let you explore the candidate's skills and experience. You can state where you feel the candidate is lacking in the required strengths and let the candidate respond to that.

5. Making the candidate speak is important. After all, you want to hear this person talk about their skills and the work they are going to do. Ask open-ended questions rather than ones that can be answered with a simple "yes" or "no."

6. Control over the interview is with you all along. You can make the transition from small talk to hard topics.

7. There are certain questions that you cannot ask legally. Equal Employment Opportunity Commission (EEOC) guidelines, as well as federal and state laws, prohibit asking certain

questions of a job applicant either on the application form or during the interview. These include such questions as:

a. Age or date of birth (if interviewing a teenager, you can ask if he or she is 16 years old)

b. Sex, sexual orientation, race, creed, color, religion, or national origin

c. Credit history

d. Disabilities of any kind

e. Date and type of military discharge

f. Marital status

8. Make notes during the interview. Do this for all candidates so that at the end of each interview, you can prepare a tabulated listing of marks and use it later to decide an order of merit.

9. Many warning signs should not be ignored unless the candidate has a very good explanation or a reason. Some of these warning signs include:

a. Arriving late for the interview

b. Treating your staff disrespectfully

c. Talking too much

d. Not wearing appropriate clothing

e. Speaking negatively about past employers

f. Asking about money too soon

g. Showing up unprepared

10. Depending on the complexity of the job being offered, you could hold several rounds of interviews. Some could be to check technical or domain knowledge, while others could be to negotiate terms and assess the suitability of the "fit." For senior appointments, there will invariably be several rounds before an offer is made.

Tools and Resources

1. SurveyMonkey - https://surveymonkey.com - Use this online solution to ask questions from candidates and create charts and graphs of the responses to help you shortlist the most promising candidates.

2. Google Hangouts - https://hangouts.google.com/ - Google makes it easy to connect with candidates, hold group discussions, and record sessions to help you make fast hiring decisions.

3. InterviewMocha - https://InterviewMocha.com - Comes with thousands of in-built skill tests that allow you to judge candidates' skills before you even get to meet them. Saves everyone a lot of time and money.

4. Spark Hire - https://www.sparkhire.com/ - A great software and mobile app for video interviews.

5. Quick hiring - http://www.quikhiring.com/ - A video interviewing tool with many benefits for both candidates and recruiters.

How to Conduct an Employee Reference Check

Why is it Important?

When you begin interacting with a prospective employee, you are essentially listening to what this person has to say. Their CV, LinkedIn profile, and Facebook page are all one-sided conversations. This person offers the information, and you listen, but the information could be incorrect or deceitfully presented.

Since the costs associated with hiring a wrong person are so large, you must make sure that the person being hired has the skills, education, temperament, and past employment history they claim to have. Extensive reference checks about the prospective employee assure you that what you've been told is correct.

During the selection process, you must inform the candidate that you will be checking references and that giving incorrect information can be grounds for rejection. Ask the prospective employee's former employers to verify skills, background, and attitudinal details. Check out the exact nature of work the candidate was doing and find out why they are switching jobs.

Sometimes people may hesitate to put things down on paper, especially if there are negative things to be said. In such a situation, use the phone to do the reference check. Putting in some effort in employee background checks will save you much time and effort in the future.

Quotes from Successful People

- *"If you pick the right people and give them the opportunity to spread their wings and put compensation as a carrier behind it, you almost don't have to manage them."* — **Jack Welch**

- *"I hire people brighter than me and I get out of their way."* — **Lee Iacocca**

- *"The competition to hire the best will increase in the years ahead. Companies that give extra flexibility to their employees will have the edge in this area."* — **Bill Gates**

- *"The secret of my success is that we have gone to exceptional lengths to hire the best people in the world."* — **Steve Jobs**

- *"Great vision without great people is irrelevant."* — **Jim Collins**

10 Great Tips

1. In the application form, you would have already received consent from the applicant to proceed with job verification and reference checks.

2. Ask for work references. Do not waste your time asking for personal references. No one will give you the names of people who will have something negative to say.

3. Do not consider the application further if the candidate refuses to supply references.

4. Check with the most recent employer first.

5. When you get a person of appropriate seniority on the line, tell him who you are and the reason for your call. Ask if you can discuss the candidate and ensure confidentiality.

6. Inform the person about the position for which the applicant is being considered so that he or she can give a more accurate evaluation of the applicant.

7. After you have given background information about the position you are looking to fill, ask some general response questions, such as "How do you think the applicant would fit into our position?" Once the person responds, ask more specific questions.

8. Let the person talk freely as long as he or she wants without interruption.

9. Watch for obvious pauses in answers. This is often a sign that further questions on the same subject may get more detailed answers.

10. Record the responses in a standardized form.

Tools and Resources

1. Haystack - https://haystack.jobs/ - Contact past employers of your candidates for free and get references checked online. Get to know more about your new hires before issuing a joining letter.

2. Checkster - http://checkster.com - Manage your entire hiring process. Check references, verify your employees, ensure correct post-interview actions, and get 360 deg feedback from almost all over the world.

3. Talytica - https://www.talytica.com - Automated reference checks with customized questions. Shorten your hiring process drastically by using this easy-to-use online tool.

4. SkillSurvey - http://www.skillsurvey.com/ - The SkillSurvey process gets you reference checks much faster than traditional methods. A large number of preset survey questions get you useful insights into candidates and ensure you hire right the first time.

5. VidCruiter - https://vidcruiter.com - Automated reference checking that makes the candidate do the hard work and gets you references anytime you want in the recruiting process. Intuitive to use with a customized workflow, it greatly improves your hiring processes.

How to Orient a New Employee

Why is it Important?

When you hire new employees, you would want them to settle down fast and become productive as soon as they can. The biggest mistake you can make is not putting in time and effort in orienting the new hire to your business's work culture and fundamental rules.

It is important to get your new employee attuned to the way of your work, the way you want them to interact with your clients, and the behavior that is expected of them. Businesses also teach new employees their basic rules about computer use, whether or not they can use their own phones for business work, and the security rules to follow.

By properly orienting a new employee, you ensure that the person is aware of the hierarchy in the office, the duties and responsibilities, and the various rules and regulations that are in force. During this process, you can also assign a mentor who will impart on the job training and the right way of working. Proper orientation for a new employee is the fastest way of making a new hire effective in your organization.

Quotes from Successful People

- *"At Google, we front-load our people investment. This means the majority of our time and money spent on people is invested in attracting, assessing, and cultivating new hires."* — **Laszlo Bock**

- *"The importance of onboarding is significantly increased these days since the average turnover at work is less than four years and lifetime employment strategies are out of date."* — **Reid Hoffman, Ben Casnocha and Chris Yeh**

- *"We want to focus on creating a memorable experience for the new hire in the first year rather than processing them in the first few weeks."* — **Cheryl Hughey**

- *"Employee orientation centers around and exists to help the individual employee, but it is the company that ultimately reaps the benefits of this practice."* — **Michael Watkins**

- *"... Once you get in, then you experience the culture and marinate in it. But now we have these orientation meetings with 10 people and it's highly likely that six of them are new. If six of them are new, you need to do something to accelerate that feeling of marinating in the culture."* — **Tawni Cranz**

10 Great Tips

1. Every employee represents an investment. How new employees are introduced to your environment will, in many ways, set the tone for how they will perform. There is no second chance to make a first impression. This applies to your company as well.

2. The new employee needs help and support to become acclimatized. If you want this process to take the least amount of time, it should be done fast and competently.

3. Good employee orientation ensures:

    a. Understanding what is important to your company

    b. Understanding the company's core values

    c. Understanding the employee's responsibilities

    d. Employee's ability to become productive faster

    e. Establishing a good working relationship

4. Taking control over the orientation and learning process is important because employees may learn the job from the wrong person.

5. Introduce the new employee to coworkers at their place of work.

6. Ideally, a manual should be given to every new employee. This manual should contain all the information you'd like the employee to know, which can be reviewed at leisure and read whenever in doubt.

7. Many organizations follow a buddy system, with new employees being given a buddy for the first few days. The selection of the buddy must be done carefully. You want to show your best employee and not someone who is unhappy.

8. Every new employee should have a general knowledge regarding the 5 Cs of your business:

    a. Customers (main customers, their demands and values)

    b. Competitors (main competitors and their strengths)

    c. Collaborators (suppliers and related businesses)

    d. Company (company history, goals, and current situation)

    e. Climate (the market, your industry)

9. Talk to the employee regarding the main issues, such as details on security, using computer networks, emailing, using the Internet, and mailing.

10. Keep in mind that a well-designed orientation program convinces new employees that they are cared for and that the company is willing to invest time and money in them.

Tools and Resources

1. Zenefit - https://www.zenefits.com/ - A total HR solution platform that is so effective for employee onboarding.

2. Click Boarding - https://www.clickboarding.com/ - A great tool to smooth your onboarding process.

3. Chief on Boarding - https://chiefonboarding.com/ - A platform to streamline your onboarding procedures. It includes various checklists and resources to make your job much easier in hiring and training new employees.

4. NASA Orientation Program – https://employeeorientation.nasa.gov/main/FirstDayExperience.htm - The checklist that NASA uses to prepare a new employee for work at the premier agency.

5. Talmundo - https://www.talmundo.com/ - An effective tool to create a great onboarding experience for your employees.

How to Train a New Employee

Why is it Important?

No matter how simple or complex your work may be, it is critical that all new employees know exactly what is expected of them and how they are supposed to work. Besides this, there are many other reasons why you must train your employees.

By training your employees, you tell them that they are valuable to you and that you are willing to put in money and effort in getting them trained. This improves employee satisfaction and confidence. In many cases, when businesses put in effort and spend money on employee training, employees tend to stay with the company for a longer time. This gives added stability to the business.

It is obvious that well-trained employees make fewer mistakes. This means less rework, fewer dissatisfied clients, and very substantial cost savings. Better trained employees directly affect the quality of your product, and this affects client retention. If you can satisfy clients, you will add substantially to your revenues.

Many businesses look at additional training as an expense, but they should look at it as an investment in employees. Well-trained employees will add to the value of the business and soon become effective contributors to earnings.

Quotes from Successful People

- *"You cannot teach people anything. You can only help them discover it within themselves."* — **Galileo**

- *"Floss only the teeth you want to keep."* — **Zig Ziglar**

- *"When you invest a dollar in a person, you get $10 back. When you invest a dollar in a machine, you get $2 back."* — **Clay Mathile**

- *"Labor looks different in the 21st century. And so should our job training programs."* — **Leila Janah**

- *"If you want to teach people a new way of thinking, don't bother trying to teach them. Instead, give them a tool, the use of which will lead to new ways of thinking."* — **R. Buckminster Fuller**

10 Great Tips

1. Training new employees well is extremely important since your new employees' productivity, safety, and organizational growth will depend on it.

2. Do not delegate the task to a trainer who is inadequately trained, lacks morale, and is not keen on the task.

3. If you do not have the right trainer, consider outsourcing the job.

4. Create training notes, job videos, and manuals that employees can refer to. Insist on creating checklists for important and complex tasks.

5. Having a good mentoring program is an effective method of improving the training and culture of your organization. Most people in your organization, even the star workers, are probably not good mentors. You must look for people who are able to establish relationships and rapport as well as command respect for their quality of work.

6. Test the employee during training sessions.

7. Break up the training into phases. New employees may not be able to grasp it all at one time. Get them back for more advanced concepts once they have mastered the basics and been on the job for some time.

8. Standardize the basic tasks.

9. Give feedback at different stages of the training classes. This will allow you to take corrective action in time.

10. Look for measurable improvement in employee performance. Know the parameters you should measure.

Tools and Resources

1. iSpring Learn - https://www.ispringsolutions.com - An easy-to-use employee onboarding and learning system that can be deployed rapidly without any programming or coding. You can create company-specific content and track the progress of your employees with ease.

2. docebo - www.docebo.com - This is a learning management system that can be customized completely to your requirements, supports 32 languages, and supports webinars, live video, documentation, and employee-paced learning.

3. Litmos - https://litmos.com - A learning platform that simplifies employee training with both prepackaged content and a content management system. It works across any networked device and provides highly customizable learning solutions.

4. AdaptiveU - https://adaptiveu.io - A learning management solution that not only trains your employees but also your

customers thereby adding greater value to your products and improving revenues.

5. Lessonly - https://www.lessonly.com/ - A free online training solution that works great for customers and employees to deliver quality content and track training and learning progress.

How to Measure Employee Performance

Why is it Important?

Business owners who are closely monitoring the performance of their business will find it essential to measure and monitor employee performance. The most obvious reason is that unless you measure employee performance, you will never know which employee to retain or promote and which employee to fire or let go.

Measuring employee performance has a direct effect on their efficiency. Employees who know they are being evaluated will take extra effort to be rated better than their peers. Besides this, by continuous evaluation, you can identify effective or noneffective employees in your organization. Once you have identified weak employees, you can put in dedicated effort to help them manage their shortcomings and become more productive.

As for employee compensation, an accurate evaluation of their performance is the only method you have to decide what they should be paid. Once employees understand that their salary is closely linked to their performance, you will find them putting in extra effort to improve workplace productivity.

Quotes from Successful People

- *"To win in the marketplace you must first win in the workplace."* — **Doug Conant**

- *"The way your employees feel is the way your customers will feel. And if your employees don't feel valued, neither will your customers."* — **Sybil F. Stershic**

- *"Highly engaged employees make the customer experience. Disengaged employees break it."* — **Timothy R. Clark**

- *"The highest levels of performance come to people who are centered, intuitive, creative, and reflective - people who know to see a problem as an opportunity."* — **Deepak Chopra**

- *"The best way to inspire people to superior performance is to convince them by everything you do and by your everyday attitude that you are wholeheartedly supporting them."* — **Harold S. Geneen**

10 Great Tips

1. A performance review is an important occasion that allows both employee and manager to establish realistic goals and expectations for the near future.

2. Managers often tend to sugarcoat problems out of hesitation or wanting to avoid unpleasant situations. While it may be important to maintain good working relationships, you will harm both your business and the employee by not being candid and open.

3. Objective and healthy feedback will help your employees grow and contribute more to the company.

4. Prepare yourself by reading the job description and the self-appraisal; consult your notes.

5. During a review, focus on both the positive and the negative aspects of the employee's performance and bring out areas where improvement is required.

6. It is important to have objective, quantifiable criteria to measure performance. Typically, these fall into areas of quality, quantity, and time.

7. Considering the quality of work, you could be measuring and discussing the following factors:

a. Customer satisfaction and feedback

b. Any complaints

c. Work output that must be redone (in percentage terms)

d. Peer perception of job performance

e. Adherence to procedures

f. Budget management

g. Attitude and behavior

h. Percentage of leads that result in sales

i. Consistency of quality

8. Be sure that you define quality norms well in advance so that all employees know what is expected of them.

9. When measuring the quantity, be careful to ensure that the quantity of work or output is qualitatively sound. The gadgets that an employee produces must be saleable. Sheer quantity without quality is only harming your business.

10. Measuring time-related issues is equally important. Can you rely on the employee to get things done on time? Does the employee coordinate complex activities with peers and customers? Is the employee punctual?

Tools and Resources

1. Zoho People - https://zoho.com/people - The complete HR solution to manage employee performance as well as many other aspects.

2. People HR - https://peoplehr.com/performance.html - An employee performance tracking tool that also focuses on getting employees to get better and improve.

3. Assess Team - https://assessteam.com - An easy-to-use, low-cost, cloud-based system that helps you manage and improve employee performance.

4. Trackstar - https://trakstar.com - A simple, easy-to-use employee evaluation solution that is ideal for small businesses.

5. Pipedrive - https://www.pipedrive.com/ - An easy-to-customize app that allows you to monitor the performance of your sales and marketing staff. See performance improvements almost immediately.

How to Communicate Effectively with Your Employees

Why is it Important?

In this age of high competition, it has become more important than ever before to have good communication with your employees. There are several reasons why. When you communicate clearly with your employees, they become aware of what is to be done and why it is required. Once they understand the reasons behind a certain action, they will be able to make the right decisions even when you are away.

There are many other advantages of effective employee communication.

- There is an immediate impact on productivity when there is open and effective communication in a business.

- It becomes easier to handle teams that could have people from different cultures and different countries.

- Good communication helps managers connect better with employees of different age groups. Managers can relate better to younger workers and understand them better.

- When you communicate openly, problems are detected earlier and solved in time before failures occur.

Quotes from Successful People

- *"Developing excellent communication skills is absolutely essential to effective leadership. The leader must be able to share knowledge and ideas to transmit a sense of urgency and enthusiasm to others. If a leader can't get a message across clearly and motivate others to act on it, then having a message doesn't even matter."* — **Gilbert Amelio**

- *"Communicate unto the other person that which you would want him to communicate unto you if your positions were reversed."* — **Aaron Goldman**

- *"The art of communication is the language of leadership."* — **James Humes**

- *"The day soldiers stop bring you their problems is the day you have stopped leading them."* — **General Colin Powell**

- *"Leaders who make it a practice to draw out the thoughts and ideas of their subordinates and who are receptive even to bad news will be properly informed. Communicate downward to subordinates with at least the same care and attention as you communicate upward to superiors."* — **L. B. Belke**

10 Great Tips

1. Sometimes we forget that employees are not mind-readers. Even the best-intentioned employees will only do what they think is effective for the company and its customers. Your job is to ensure that what the employee thinks is the best is really so.

2. Clear job descriptions and management expectations help to remove doubts.

3. Goals must be SMART—specific, measurable, achievable, realistic, and timely.

4. Do everything possible to get your team on the same page as you are.

5. Setting performance expectations will be easier if you clarify the list below for your employees:

a. What does a good job look like? Which results are satisfactory, and which are great?

b. Why, what, and how to do the job.

c. How is an employee expected to behave when performing a task?

d. How long should it take to complete the job?

e. Which are the likely safety issues?

f. How can the job be performed in an economical manner?

g. Does any company or other rules or regulations affect how the job should be performed?

6. Even when you are communicating extensively, make sure that the message reaching all employees is the message you are seeking to give. For example, you may do something to save money, while employees may take it to mean their jobs are not secure.

7. Communication mismatch can occur for various reasons, including the following:

a. Varying frames of reference

b. Varying listening skills and distractions

c. Personal variables, such as emotional state or prejudice

8. You will need to obtain regular and extensive feedback to ensure that all your employees are getting your messages correctly. Failure to do so could lead to nasty surprises.

9. Check back with your employees as to what they think you want them to do. This is called checking receipt of communication (ROC). You will be surprised at the variation you will sometimes hear even if you have just given out instructions. Use the opportunity to improve your messages so that ambiguity is eliminated.

10. Spoken instructions are often interpreted differently because most employees will forget exactly what has been said and will work with the instructions as they remember them. For the critical jobs, create a written instruction, which will ensure

that even after several days, the employee can refer back to it, and this reduces the chances of making a mistake.

Tools and Resources

1. Brosix - https://brosix.com - An encrypted instant manager that is closely tailored to business needs. Handles chat, file and screen sharing, and many more features.

2. Yammer - https://yammer.com - A collaborative and community-based communication tool for communication within businesses.

3. Basecamp - https://basecamp.com - A team communication solution that cuts down the need to hold meetings by more than 50%. Gets everyone on the same page, fast.

4. Fuze - https://www.fuze.com/ - A team communication solution built with an eye on remote workforces in different offices. Real-time data and screen sharing and HD playback ensure great communication.

5. Google Hangouts Chat - https://gsuite.google.com/products/chat/ - If your company uses the Google application suite, then Hangouts Chat is essential. It is completely integrated with other Google productivity tools and will take business communication to a different level.

How to Retain Good Employees

Why is it Important?

It is critical not to lose your good employees if you are serious about growing your business. To begin with, stability in your workforce is very good for your business. It means that you are not constantly having to train new employees and search for specialized talent. Retaining good employees for as long as possible is essential to growth. Employees who have been with you for a long time get accustomed to your work and are able to generate new ideas and suggestions. This is not possible with employees who come and go.

A stable workforce leads to strong teams. If people are happy working for you and there is a friendly environment at work, you will find good teamwork in the workplace. This ensures that people support each other and handle emergencies collectively.

Rapid employee turnover worries customers too. They can see when people change too rapidly. Customers can then get worried over whether or not their work will be done well by temporary employees.

While it is not possible to have zero employee turnover, keeping it low makes good business sense.

Quotes from Successful People

- *"Always treat your employees exactly as you want them to treat your best customers."* — **Stephen R. Covey**

- *"Employees who believe that management is concerned about them as a whole person—not just an employee—are more productive, more satisfied, more fulfilled. Satisfied employees mean satisfied customers, which leads to profitability."* — **Anne Mulcahy**

- *"Dispirited, unmotivated, unappreciated workers cannot compete in a highly competitive world."* — **Francis Hesselbein**

- *"When people go to work, they shouldn't have to leave their hearts at home."* — **Betty Bender**

- *"Create caring and robust connections between every employee and their work, customers, leaders, managers, and the organization to achieve results that matter to everyone in this sentence."* — **David Zinger**

10 Great Tips

1. It is not easy to find good employees, and we have seen how effective good employees are to a successful business.

2. If you hired good employees, the next step is ensuring that they continue to work for you with their heart and soul and are not waiting for the right time to switch to one of your competitors.

3. There is much you can do to retain employees and build a happy, hardworking, and innovative team. Monetary compensation is a small part of it.

4. Much of your employee retention depends on the quality of communication with your employees.

5. Share your vision with your staff. What is critical is that employees know very clearly what the company stands for, how it is moving toward its goals, and where the employee fits in.

6. Share success and defeats: There will be a fair share of both. Sharing them with your employees will prepare them for the bad times and help them build on the good ones.

7. Top employees look for opportunities. Top employees also need mentoring and feedback.

8. Provide plenty of positive feedback to average employees every time they grow a little.

9. Use challenges, the workplace environment, and recognition to motivate your employees.

10. Be fair to your employees!

Tools and Resources

1. iAppreciate - https://iappreciate.com/ - An application that helps you celebrate employee successes and share them with your workforce.

2. Achievers - https://www.achievers.com/what-we-offer/ - This is an employee recognition platform that helps you keep your staff motivated and leads to better employee retention figures.

3. TerryBerry - https://www.terryberry.com/360-recognition-platform/ - This is a 360 deg recognition platform that combines all corporate recognition platforms that your company has. You get better employee retention with all your recognition programs working in synergy with each other.

4. Teamphoria - http://www.sparcet.com/ - This easy-to-use solution encourages employee-to-employee recognition. This leads to a happier workplace where coworkers bond better and build strong and productive teams.

5. Globoforce - https://www.globoforce.com/products/social-recognition/ - Improve employee retention by using this proven employee engagement solution. Better collaboration and communication improve innovation and creativity.

How to Give Bonuses and Rewards to Employees

Why is it Important?

All of us love gifts, and more so if they are unexpected ones. Used well, bonuses can be very encouraging and satisfying for your employees, and you may end up getting back far more than what you have paid out. Bonuses also make employees work harder in anticipation and will often improve employee loyalty to the company.

Bonuses can be monetary or nonmonetary. They can be linked to the profit your company makes or to individual employee performance. In many cases, companies give out a year-end bonus as an incentive to all employees as a mark of gratitude and employee welfare. When giving bonuses, it is important to be fair and give out bonuses in accordance with a clear policy and measurement criteria so that no one feels they have been overlooked.

Although bonuses may not help directly in employee retention, they do tell your employees that they are wanted and that their work is being noticed. As a result, employees feel that management is concerned about them and values their effort. This leads directly to better employee relationships, a happier business environment, and satisfied workers.

Quotes from Successful People

- *"People work for money but go the extra mile for recognition, praise and rewards."* — **Dale Carnegie**

- *"Brains, like hearts, go where they are appreciated."* — **Robert McNamara**

- *"An employee's motivation is a direct result of the sum of interactions with his or her manager."* — **Dr. Bob Nelson**

- *"Motivation is the art of getting people to do what you want them to do because they want to do it."* — **Dwight D. Eisenhower**

- *"Recognition is the greatest motivator."* — **Gerard C. Eakedale**

10 Great Tips

1. A bonus is a form of performance-related pay, and there are advantages both for and against giving bonuses.

2. While bonuses have a motivating effect on the person who gets it, there could be adverse reactions from those who don't.

3. Bonuses work well with jobs that can be easily measured, such as production on the shop floor.

4. You will need to decide in advance what the bonus amount can be and allocate accordingly.

5. Some examples of circumstances where bonuses could be paid:

   a. Salespersons exceeding quotas

   b. Innovations for improving processes and increasing savings

   c. Attracting new customers

    d. Exceeding collections

    e. Finishing projects ahead of time or under budget

    f. Working substantially more than required

6. The rewards must be carefully chosen. They must meet the following criteria:

    a. Should be consistent with the corporate message and company goals

    b. Be very clearly tied to job performance

    c. Be very fairly selected

    d. Be distinct from pay and other privileges

7. Why not ask your employees themselves how they want to be recognized? You will get many great ideas and suggestions.

8. Make sure that the award does not become routine, or it will lose its value.

9. Here are some ideas you can use to appreciate your employees:

    a. Give an extra day off

    b. Gift cards or coupons

    c. Tickets to a show or a game

    d. Pinning a congratulatory poster on the office notice board

    e. Give a monogrammed mug filled with candy

    f. Gifts, such as laptop bags and briefcases

10. All rewards must be clearly tied to job performance.

Tools and Resources

1. Bonusly - https://bonus.ly - With this platform, everyone in your organization can recognize talent and give anyone else a small bonus. It all adds up to big productivity gains.

2. Wishlist Rewards - https://wishlistrewards.com - Give your employees the rewards they appreciate and work toward using Wishlist Rewards.

3. Guudjob - https://guudjob.com - This employee reward solution incorporates customer feedback, peer review, and manager inputs to create 360-degree feedback that helps improve work culture.

4. Disco - https://justdisco.com - Disco works within teams and helps team members appreciate each other's work and successes and improve team productivity.

5. Achievers - https://www.achievers.com/ - An effective platform for inspiring and rewarding employees.

How to Create a Great Team

Why is it Important?

Teamwork among your employees can be a real force multiplier. In a good team, everyone supports each other, and people work together to help in case there is an emergency. The pace of work in a well-knit team is far better than in a group that is not cohesive and does not work well together. People feel more secure in a good team and are not hesitant about offering ideas and suggestions. This helps your business handle tougher projects and more difficult tasks.

Great teams are not formed at random. Management is very important in developing strong teamwork in the company. Management that is fair, transparent, and values a supportive work environment will be able to build strong teams in the company. In such an environment, employees share information and help build solutions rather than simply guarding their own turf.

Quotes from Successful People

- *"Teamwork is the ability to work together toward a common vision. The ability to direct individual accomplishments toward organizational objectives. It is the fuel that allows common people to attain uncommon results."* — **Andrew Carnegie**

- *"Coming together is a beginning, staying together is progress, and working together is success."* — **Henry Ford**

- *"Find a group of people who challenge and inspire you, spend a lot of time with them, and it will change your life."* — **Amy Poehler**

- *"Teamwork begins by building trust. And the only way to do that is to overcome our need for invulnerability."* — **Patrick Lencioni**

- *"Great things in business are never done by one person; they're done by a team of people."* — **Steve Jobs**

10 Great Tips

1. Teams should go through various stages of
   a. Defining goals and the purpose of team creation
   b. Adding members and defining their roles
   c. Solving conflicts among team members
   d. Smoothing procedures and developing a great working environment
   e. Reviewing and improving team performance

2. Diversity is the key to having a successful team. You need people with various skills and mindsets based on your purpose.

3. Develop a great relationship with your team members. Learn about their personal and professional values.

4. Be clear about your team goals and missions.

5. Create a great environment so that your team members can share their ideas and opinions.

6. Encourage your team members to ask questions and to be asked by other members.

7. Involve all members in the decision-making process. People are more engaged when they have a sense of ownership in the projects.

8. Have regular meetings with your team to review performance and share the issues.

9. Appreciate your team's hard work and coach them to improve themselves.

10. Conflicts happen, but the way you solve them is important. Consider each conflict as an opportunity for further development.

Tools and Resources

1. Goosechase - http://www.goosechase.com/ - Encourage competitiveness and build strong teams within your employees. Build teams while having fun.

2. GoGame - http://www.thegogame.com - A team-building game that includes a lot of social sharing among your employees.

3. iMeet - https://www.pgi.com/webcasting-webinars-software/ - Get your people together virtually! Host online meetings and events without any stress at all. Build teams even when the members are separated geographically.

4. Scavify - https://www.scavify.com/teambuilding - Break the ice - introduce your employees to a fun environment where they get to know each other and improve collaboration.

5. Timely - https://timelyapp.com/ - A great app for team building, time tracking, and performance evaluating.

How to Pay Your Employees Properly

Why is it Important?

It is important to pay your employees properly. You need to pay them well, on time, and what they were promised. There are both ethical and practical reasons to do this.

The ethical reasons are clear. If an employee has worked for you, you are technically under their debt, and the only way you can clear it is by paying them what was promised. On the practical front, it is very obvious that the organization only exists because its employees put in the effort to create the output that the owner has thought of. If the business did not have competent employees to work in it, there would have been no product, no revenue, no profits, and very soon, no business. You also need to pay your employees a fair wage because there are a number of regulations covering this issue, and getting involved in needless litigation is best avoided.

With the spread of the Internet, it has become very easy for employees to compare salaries and find out if other employers are offering better salaries for the same skills. This can easily lead to a situation where you lose a skilled workforce. The loss to your business can be enormous. This can be avoided by paying your employees well.

Quotes from Successful People

- *"Paying your employees well is not only the right thing to do but it makes for good business."* — **James Sinegal**

- *"It is difficult to get a man to understand something when his salary depends upon his not understanding it."* — **Upton Sinclair**

- *"It was definitely not the salary that made me join Manchester United; I went for football reasons—for the history of the club, the league, the fans, and the coach because he is one of the best in the world."* — **Henrikh Mkhitaryan**

- *"'What is your desired salary?' The unwritten rule when it comes to salary is this: whoever proposes a number first loses. When you interview, you should never feel pressured to answer this question. Simply let your interviewer know that the most important thing to you is how well you fit the position."* — **Travis Bradberry**

- *"People are still willing to do an honest day's work. The trouble is they want a week's pay for it."* — **Joey Adams**

10 Great Tips

1. Pay and performance are closely linked because, to a large extent, one determines the other.

2. There is much involved in employee motivation besides pay. Ensure compensation has nothing to do with gender, race, sexual preference, religion, or nationality. When in doubt, imagine explaining your stand to a court.

3. Employee compensation is one of the largest expenses of the company. It also has an important role in employee perceptions of the company since it sends a message about what standards of work and performance are desirable.

4. Compensation can also be an emotional issue with many people when you are assessing their self-worth in terms of a paycheck.

5. Whether or not the company is fair to its employees will also depend on the company's salary structure.

6. Compensation needs to be based on the three parameters of job accountability, goal attainment, and value-added functions.

7. Job accountability: whether or not the employee is meeting the requirements that were described when the employee was hired

8. Goal attainment: whether or not employees are able to meet their own goals

9. Value-added functions: such as good communication, building relationships with clients, maintaining a positive attitude, and going out of the way to help the business

10. Compensation also needs to take into account the location of the business, the experience level of the employee, and salary levels of similar employees in the company, and similar businesses in the vicinity.

Tools and Resources

1. Intuit - https://www.intuit.com/- A payroll solution that is guaranteed to calculate accurate payrolls and taxes.

2. Onpay - https://payrollcenter.com/onpay/ - A payroll and payment solution for small businesses that is economical and easy to use.

3. Gusto - https://gusto.com/ - A pay and accounting system for small businesses that will give your past employees access to their information, pay stubs, and W-2s—even after they've left your company.

4. Sage - https://www.sage.com - A payroll solution that grows with the size of your business. Retain records forever with this cloud-based solution.

5. SurePayroll - https://www.surepayroll.com/ - Do you have a home-based business? Or maybe a restaurant or a nonprofit? SurePayroll is just right for these offbeat requirements.

How to Make an Effective Change in Your Organization

Why is it Important?

Your organization has to evolve with changing circumstances and market conditions. Smart businesses are willing to adapt and make changes as the situation changes in the marketplace. Changes may also be required if the technology you use develops and evolves. In this case, if you are slow to adapt, you could lose out on business opportunities. In many cases, changes in regulations will require you to change your methods of work.

When you make changes, you must also manage the disruption and the rate of change to ensure that your employees can accept the changes being made.

While some changes are necessary and critical, sometimes businesses make cosmetic changes or just pretend to change just to put up a show of being with the times. Merely changing the packing box without changing the product inside may not lead to success. Beware of these so-called improvements. They only give the impression of change without actually leading to any improvement. Smart businesses handle change well.

Quotes from Successful People

- *"Change before you have to."* — **Jack Welch**

- *"The greatest danger in times of turbulence is not the turbulence—it is to act with yesterday's logic."* — **Peter Drucker**

- *"Change is hard because people overestimate the value of what they have and underestimate the value of what they may gain by giving that up."* — **James Belasco and Ralph Stayer**

- *"Never doubt that a small group of thoughtful, concerned citizens can change the world. Indeed it is the only thing that ever has."* — **Margaret Mead**

- *"It is not the strongest or the most intelligent who will survive but those who can best manage change."* — **Charles Darwin**

10 Great Tips

1. Let's face it! We all like certainty, and no one likes change—more so when the reasons for change are not made clear. Your employees will not like change either.

2. While you may have the most compelling reasons for the change, unless you get your employees on board, the change is not going to be successful.

3. When faced with a change situation, remember that the employee may not have the input you have and may be wondering why the change is needed. To get their support, you need to convince them.

4. Employees need to be reassured that the change is not going to hurt them.

5. Employees resist change because of various reasons:

    a. They do not understand what the change involves

    b. They do not understand how it will affect them

    c. They do not understand the reason behind the change

6. When you have to implement a change that is large and likely to cause worry, take the time to talk to your employees in detail.

7. Speak to them in small groups so that you can talk to them individually and give them detailed reasons for the change and what it involves.

8. Be sure to give them the opportunity to ask as many questions as they wish.

9. If your reasons are logical and convincing, these employees will spread the word and convince others.

10. Successful organizations are those in which individuals are encouraged to challenge the main assumptions and think out of the box to improve their personal and organizational skills.

Tools and Resources

1. WhatFix - https://whatfix.com/ - An ideal tool for change management, user support, and employee training management. Simplify business management.

2. OrgMapper - https://www.orgmapper.com/ - Discover the influencers in your company and work through them to simplify change management.

3. Nakisa - https://www.nakisa.com - Stay on top of organizational change management issues with this agile and low-risk solution.

4. Change Compass - https://www.thechangecompass.com/ - Change Compass helps organizations manage change by clearly defining the impact on staff and customers. The solution also comes with in-built best practices to manage organizational change effectively.

5. Peakon - https://peakon.com - A great tool to involve employees in change management and share their feedback to improve your business.

How to Deal with a Complacent Employee

Why is it Important?

Employee complacency can cost you a lot in lost opportunities, revenue, and productivity. You need to catch it as it is developing and not leave the correction too late. A complacent employee who is not corrected in time can affect several others who may learn from the wrong example they see. As a result, you may reach a situation where the overall culture of the business becomes complacent and too easygoing. This is bound to hurt your business.

It is important to deal with a complacent employee quickly before the disease spreads across your company. This will help you save many more employees who may be wanting to copy the complacent behavior.

It is important to sit down and talk with the complacent employee and discuss your concerns. Tell this person what part of their behavior is not up to standard and what should be done to improve it. In many cases, this is all that is required. Sometimes the employee may not even be aware of the problem, and a few words of advice may make a big difference. Improving your employees' performance is one of the major parts of your responsibilities as the owner/manager of your small business.

Quotes from Successful People

- *"Competition is always a good thing. It forces us to do our best. A monopoly renders people complacent and satisfied with mediocrity."* — **Nancy Pearcey**

- *"I think it's dangerous to think that you're successful, because then you become complacent."* — **Tommy Hilfiger**

- *"I think it's good to have pressure on yourself. The worst crime is to get kind of really complacent."* — **Edgar Wright**

- *"Being complacent was never going to teach us anything."* — **Bonnie Hammer**

- *"It is nice to be around people who think differently than you. They challenge your ideas and keep you from being complacent."* — **Tucker Carlson**

10 Great Tips

1. Complacency can occur if employees are too settled and comfortable in their job.

2. Even though some employees may want to work effectively, the organizational culture may prevent them from doing their best.

3. Less communication between managers and employees leads to complacency.

4. Lack of challenge in a job that has become routine is another major reason.

5. Your job as a manager is to ensure this does not happen. That does not mean that you keep people off balance and uncomfortable; some managers do try that with disastrous results.

6. You can break complacency by providing a degree of challenge in a job. If a job takes thirty minutes, challenge your staff to cut five minutes regularly.

7. Ask if they can change the process to make the procedure more efficient or use fewer resources.

8. Keep them thinking, and when you do get an employee to do something spectacular, remember to give reward and positive feedback.

9. Break the monotony by well-planned activities and rotate employees between jobs wherever possible.

10. These changes also provide cross-training. Not only do your employees appreciate one another's work, but you will also have a cross-trained employee.

Tools and Resources

1. Book: *The Golden Rules of Human Resource Management: What Every Manager Ought to Know*, by Ali Asadi
https://amzn.to/2LcLtyN

2. Book: *The Essential HR Handbook, 10th Anniversary Edition: A Quick and Handy Resource for Any Manager or HR Professional*, by Sharon Armstrong and Barbara Mitchell
https://amzn.to/2L91Jkb

3. Book: *SHRM Essential Guide to Employment Law*, by Charles Fleischer https://amzn.to/2NwG600

4. Book: *The Little Black Book of Human Resources Management*, by Barry Wolfe https://amzn.to/2MClljW

5. Book: *HR on Purpose: Developing Deliberate People Passion*, by Steve Browne https://amzn.to/2MDyc5l

How to Give Feedback to Your Employees

Why is it Important?

Even though you may be busy running your business, you have to find time to give the necessary feedback to your employees. Feedback is not only the corrective action you implement when things are not going well, but it also includes a pat on the back and a word of praise. Employees who get regular (and honest) feedback about their performance tend to care more about their work and the well-being of the business. This is because most people appreciate the effort managers take in giving them an appraisal of how things are going. It gives them a feeling of purpose and belonging. Employees who get regular feedback also feel that their work is worthwhile and that management genuinely cares for them.

Feedback can flow both ways. When you have an employee in areas where you think improvements need to be made, you should also be looking at getting information and feedback from the employee. This will help you remove the bottlenecks that may be affecting your business, and that may be preventing the employee from giving their best. This kind of useful conversation is only possible if you initiate the discussion and encourage the employee to respond and give you their inputs as well.

Quotes from Successful People

- *"We all need people who will give us feedback. That's how we improve."* — **Bill Gates**

- *"I think it's very important to have a feedback loop, where you're constantly thinking about what you've done and how you could be doing it better."* — **Elon Musk**

- *"There is a huge value in learning with instant feedback."* — **Anant Agarwal**

- *"Negative feedback is better that none. I would rather have a man hate me than overlook me. As long as he hates me I make a difference."* — **Hugh Prather**

- *"By maintaining an active feedback system at every stage of a startup, founders can reduce their burn rate, increase their virality coefficient, and retain key hires."* — **Jay Samit**

10 Great Tips

1. It has been proven that one of the main reasons for employees leaving a company is poor communication and a feeling that their efforts are not appreciated.

2. As soon as practical, you must give feedback to your employees about their standards of performance, which includes both good and bad news.

3. Giving feedback is an art you must develop. Your interest is only in the development of employees and improvement in their standards of work.

4. By giving your employees positive feedback (when deserved), you show them that:

    a. You are attentive to what they do and how they do it.

    b. Their efforts are appreciated.

    c. They are further encouraged to perform better.

    d. Their actions are reinforced.

5. Do not, however, go to the other extreme and give lavish, false praise.

6. Give positive feedback in public and negative feedback in private.

7. Be timely. Try to give positive feedback immediately after noticing a certain activity; give negative feedback within twenty-four hours. The difference is because you are giving

positive strokes publicly, and you do not need to wait for a specific time.

8. Focus on behavior, not the person. Instead of saying, "you are habitually careless," say, "you have damaged the equipment."

9. Be sure of your facts. Take some time to check in case you have any doubt.

10. Encourage your customers to give good feedback to your employees as well.

Tools and Resources

1. Slack - https://slack.com/ - An effective tool for organizational communication. Offers both group and one on one chat and videoconferencing. Handle many different projects and collaborate with ease using this versatile tool.

2. Atlassian - https://www.atlassian.com/ - Offers a range of collaborative features as well as tight integration with Salesforce, Dropbox, and many other productivity tools.

3. Microsoft Teams - https://products.office.com/en-us/microsoft-teams/group-chat-software - Focuses on real-time collaboration between employees, feedback, and team activities and links closely with your Office 365 account to improve your productivity.

4. Flowdock - http://www.flowdock.com/ - Flowdock is a chat and in-box manager that allows you to keep all employee conversations in one place. This improves project management, customer support, and employee feedback and tasking.

5. Facebook Workplace - https://work.facebook.com - Specifically designed for better business communication, Facebook Workplace offers group conversations, screen sharing, broadcasting, and private chat that you can use to provide employee feedback.

How to Give Benefits and Perks to Employees

Why is it Important?

Interviews with a large number of job seekers routinely show that benefit packages and perks are particularly important as to how employees view companies as a good place to work. Since all businesses work hard to attract top-notch talent, the benefits and perks they offer become an important part of the overall package being given to employees.

When you plan the benefits package, remember that one size does not fit all. Employees of different age groups are motivated differently. The older generation looks for stability and salary. The younger generation looks for work/life balance, quality of life, and flexible work.

If you have a generous benefits package, you can use it to hire better candidates. Your overall compensation package looks more attractive and will attract more qualified candidates if the benefits are attractive. Businesses often post these benefits on their careers portal. Good benefits and an attractive salary help reduce the turnover of employees. This brings stability to your business and reduces the cost of continuously having to train new employees.

Quotes from Successful People

- *"The simple act of paying positive attention to people has a great deal to do with productivity."* — **Tom Peters**

- *"Dispirited, unmotivated, unappreciated workers cannot compete in a highly competitive world."* — **Francis Hesselbein**

- *"Research indicates that workers have three prime needs: Interesting work, recognition for doing a good job, and being let in on things that are going on in the company."* — **Zig Ziglar**

- *"The way your employees feel is the way your customers will feel. And if your employees don't feel valued, neither will your customers."* — **Sybil F. Stershic**

- *"The simple act of paying positive attention to people has a great deal to do with productivity."* — **Tom Peters**

10 Great Tips

1. Benefits differ from other motivators in that they are not aligned to performance but are made available to every employee.

2. These can include insurance, medical, sick leave, paid leave, overtime rates, and retirement savings plans.

3. These are made available to every employee who meets specified criteria, such as being with the company for more than a certain number of days or working more than a specified number of hours per week.

4. Whatever you do, ensure that the benefits criteria is available on the internal website (or manual) of the company. It is also applied fairly and transparently.

5. You will gain more overall by being fair than by giving too many benefits to a few star performers.

6. A bonus is a form of performance-related pay, and there are advantages both for and against giving bonuses.

7. While bonuses have a motivating effect on the person who gets it, there could be adverse reactions from those who don't. For this reason, many companies do not publicize the bonuses they pay.

8. You will need to decide in advance what the bonus amount can be and allocate accordingly.

9. Numerous surveys have shown that employees want recognition and appreciation more than anything else.

10. Why not ask your employees themselves how they want to be recognized? You will get many great ideas and suggestions.

Tools and Resources

1. PeopleKeep - https://www.peoplekeep.com - PeopleKeep gives you smart, new ways of giving your employees benefits that keep them motivated and do not add to their tax liability. Happy employees mean better work.

2. Perks at Work - https://www.perksatwork.com - A portal that is solely dedicated to employee perks and their management. Employers can choose from hundreds of ready-to-deploy perks at no cost to their company.

3. Next Jump - https://www.nextjump.com/ - A free platform that puts together more than 30,000 discounts you can offer your staff. It also comes with an employee recognition module you can use to keep your staff motivated.

4. Book: *The Vibrant Workplace: Overcoming the Obstacles to Building a Culture of Appreciation*, by Dr. Paul White and Gary Chapman https://amzn.to/2U3cjNP

5. Book: *The 5 Languages of Appreciation in the Workplace: Empowering Organizations by Encouraging People*, by Gary Chapman and Paul White https://amzn.to/323Qe4d

How to Discipline and Fire an Employee

Why is it Important?

Disciplining employees is an important HR activity that must not be overlooked or delayed. The aim is to correct employee behavior in time rather than allowing a situation to develop where more drastic action is required to be taken. Supervisors must explain what improvements are required and how they must be implemented.

By taking timely disciplinary action against an employee, you protect other hardworking employees in your organization. Once the redlines are made clear, and the rules are applied fairly and transparently, all employees understand what is expected of them. This guidance is important and ensures good employee behavior.

Once in a while, there will be an employee who does not respond to discipline. In such cases, it is wiser to fire the employee. However, you must document the counseling and the warnings that have been given previously so that your actions can stand independent scrutiny.

Quotes from Successful People

- *"Discipline is the bridge between goals and accomplishment."* — **Jim Rohn**

- *"Discipline is the soul of an army. It makes small numbers formidable; procures success to the weak, and esteem to all."* — **George Washington**

- *"The only discipline that lasts is self-discipline."* — **Bum Philips**

- *"Discipline is remembering what you want."* — **David Campbell**

- *"You have to be responsible when you're running an organization, and firing people who are your friends is part of that responsibility."* — **Ben Horowitz**

10 Great Tips

1. As much as you'd hate it, this is also part of the job, and at some time or another, you may be called upon to do.

2. The disciplining process is not creating grounds for dismissal; rather, it is attempting to correct the behavior that is causing a problem.

3. There is a human aspect to the process. You want to keep the procedure dignified and mature.

4. There is a legal element as well. The actions you take could be challenged in court.

5. Disciplinary action could take the form of verbal counseling, which could be followed up with a written warning if no improvement occurs and more severe action if necessary.

6. Verbal counseling. Record the event and the points discussed in the employee's file. Record date and time, and people present.

7. Warning notices are very important documents and will often be required to be presented in court.

8. Retain copies of all warnings in the employee's file.

9. You must ensure that the employee is given adequate time between two such notices so that behavior can be changed and for results to be seen.

10. Do not forget to consult with a lawyer if you are in doubt.

Tools and Resources

1. The Society for Human Resource Management (SHRM) - https://www.shrm.org- One of the most comprehensive resources to answer all your HR needs.

2. Patriot Software - https://www.patriotsoftware.com/ - If you are terminating an employee, this termination checklist will help you avoid the pitfalls in the process.

3. Better team - https://www.betterteam.com/ - The employee termination letter is an important legal document. You must also ensure that it is fair and humane. This great resource gives you several templates for a termination letter.

4. Book: *101 Sample Write-Ups for Documenting Employee Performance Problems: A Guide to Progressive Discipline & Termination*, by Paul Falcone https://amzn.to/326jkjl

5. Book: *Effective Phrases for Performance Appraisals: A Guide to Successful Evaluations*, by James E. Neal Jr. https://amzn.to/2UbwOba

How to Delegate Tasks

Why is it Important?

Effective managers understand how critical it is to be able to delegate their work effectively. By distributing work to competent staff and partners, they can supervise more and able to plan in depth. Delegating work also helps the manager task staff according to their capabilities. This ensures that the manager can devote complete attention to the critical tasks that can only be performed by the manager. Delegation of work also saves the manager from micromanaging every aspect of work in the office.

Delegating responsibilities to subordinates is also empowering for the subordinates. Once you involve your employees in more complex tasks, they feel important and begin to take more responsibility. This improves the quality of your workforce.

Allowing your employees to work independently also gives you an opportunity to assess them and prepares them for future roles. This slowly builds the second tier of managers and gives great stability to the business.

Quotes from Successful People

- *"The inability to delegate is one of the biggest problems I see with managers at all levels."* — **Eli Broad**

- *"I always delegate. If someone is very good at something, whatever it is, he will be in charge."* — **Johan Cruyff**

- *"When you delegate work to the member of the team, your job is to clearly frame success and describe the objectives."* — **Steven Sinofsky**

- *"You can delegate authority, but you cannot delegate responsibility."* — **Byron Dorgan**

- *"I think one of my strengths is that I can always take advice, and I can delegate. I know a lot of people feel the need to do everything themselves, but I am not one of them."* — **Dasha Zhukova**

10 Great Tips

1. Successful managers are often masters of delegation.

2. You can never be good at everything your business requires to be done.

3. If you have chosen your employees with care and have trained them well, you should be able to delegate to them. Any executive who attempts to do everything himself will soon get caught up in the details and will lose sight of the big picture.

4. Be very clear about what the job is and how it is to be done.

5. Brief your subordinates very clearly.

6. Allow freedom to work; accept that different people do the same job differently.

7. Keep track of what is happening, but don't breathe down their necks.

8. You can delegate a job, but the responsibility stays with you.

9. Do not delegate jobs that involve bad news or have a high degree of uncertainty.

10. Do not delegate if the risk is high.

Tools and Resources

1. Ontraport - https://ontraport.com/ - Plan your work and business campaigns visually, delegate your tasks to the right person, and get a timely follow-up.

2. Trello - https://trello.com/ - Work with Trello's boards, cards, and to-do lists to delegate work effectively and keep track of timelines and task status.

3. Producteev - https://www.producteev.com/ - A task management solution that helps you stay on top of your work and delegate your work effectively.

4. Delegation Calculator - http://transcendengagement.com/ - How effective is your delegation? Are you getting the desired results? Check out the delegation calculator; many other useful resources and downloadable tools are available from this website.

5. Book: *Delegation and Supervision*, by Brain Tracy https://amzn.to/2HFOWF9

How to Create a Great Work Manual for Your Business

Why is it Important?

As your business grows, it is important to move away from ad hoc ways of working and moving to more formalized procedures. Creating "standard operating procedures" and work manuals is a great way of ensuring structured work in your business.

With a small business, the owner is able to monitor the work fairly closely. As the business grows, however, the owner is unable to devote significant time to all aspects of the work. Under such circumstances, it pays to identify all routine work and create detailed work manuals for these. Once the work manual is understood and accepted, work on that aspect happens automatically, and the manager/owner need only ensure periodically that the manual is being followed. This reduces the workload on the manager and allows this person to take on more strategic work.

Creating work manuals also ensures that all important components of the activity are listed, and no activity is overlooked. Eventually, as your business stabilizes, you must try and get as much of your work as possible into a routine pattern. Work manuals are a great way of ensuring this.

Quotes from Successful People

- *"If you can't describe what you are doing as a process, you don't know what you are doing."* — **W. Edwards Deming**

- *"Chaos is NOT a condition of doing business."* — **Karen Martin**

- *"Having and understanding of the 'why' will help having an understanding of the 'how.'"* — **Bobby Darnell**

- *"Processes underpin business capabilities, and capabilities underpin strategy execution."* — **Pearl Zhu**

- *"Almost all quality improvement comes via simplification of design, manufacturing layout, processes, and procedures."* — **Tom Peters**

10 Great Tips

1. The operational manual is a reference handbook to define various working procedures of your business to train and manage employees.

2. This manual may include contact lists, how-to guides, checklists, policies, frequently asked questions, and sample letterforms.

3. The operational manual should have a table of contents with the main sections.

4. Start the manual with basic information and add different sections based on your type of business.

5. Ask your current staff, other stakeholders, and professional consultants to help you in writing and reviewing your manual.

6. The operational manual is a living document that should be improved or updated regularly.

7. You should have regular meetings with your staff to review and improve your operational manual.

8. Make your manual simple to use and friendly. Keep in mind that complexity is the enemy of implementation.

9. Ask all new employees to read the operational manual before starting their work.

10. Create an online version of your operational manual as well so that it can be accessed by your employees easily.

Tools and Resources

1. Manula - https://www.manula.com/ - Create manuals, embed video and images, format to your exact specifications, and convert to pdf and publish. Manula gives you high-quality, low-priced document management capability.

2. PolicyHub - https://www.mitratech.com/products/policyhub/ - Complete life cycle management of all your company policies and manuals. It ensures ease of work and easy dissemination of policies to all your employees.

3. NETConsent - http://www.netconsent.com/products-services/compliance-suite - Manage the entire set of your policy guidelines, manuals, forms, and procedures from this single interface. This system greatly simplifies your business tasks.

4. 360factors - http://www.360factors.com/ - Management of manuals, guidelines, and documentation across a large number of different domains. Look for information specific to your vertical and manage your manuals with ease.

5. ProProfs - https://www.proprofs.com/knowledgebase/ - Improve the quality of your manuals and ensure that your employees and customers find the information they need quickly and accurately. Keep the information public or private as per your need and access it from anywhere.

How to Prevent Employee Theft and Fraud

Why is it Important?

Several studies have shown that businesses may lose as much as 10 percent of their revenue due to employee theft and fraud. If you were generating 10 percent additional revenue, you could afford to lower prices and gain market share or perhaps improve your product further or maybe even pay yourself a bit more. One way to ensure additional revenue is by preventing theft by employees.

Owners who do not take corrective action to stop theft put the future of their business in danger. Other employees notice the ongoing theft and might be encouraged to do the same. You need to take prompt corrective action to ensure that the right message is sent to all employees.

You can take several steps to check theft and fraud. Good internal procedures, proper accounting of equipment and funds, and frequent checks are necessary to ensure that theft and fraud are minimized. As the owner/manager, it is your responsibility to show that this is something you are extremely serious about and will not accept any kind of unethical behavior by your employees.

Quotes from Successful People

- *"If we don't act now to safeguard our privacy, we could all become victims of identity theft."* — **Bill Nelson**

- *"When dealing with people, remember you are not dealing with creatures of logic, but creatures of emotion."* — **Dale Carnegie**

- *"There are three things in the world that deserve no mercy, hypocrisy, fraud, and tyranny."* — **Frederick William Robertson**

- *"Corruption is like a ball of snow, once it's set a rolling it must increase."* — **Charles Caleb Colton**

- *"There is no compromise when it comes to corruption. You have to fight it."* — **A. K. Antony**

10 Great Tips

1. Employee fraud and theft pose a great risk to the success of any business.

2. Careful attention should be paid to designing and implementing internal controls because their absence may lead to an organizational environment that serves as a hotbed for fraudulent activity.

3. Management should try to foster a positive work environment since it leads to job satisfaction.

4. Fair policies, open communication in all directions, informal work practices, decentralized authority, and a more flexible organizational structure all contribute to a positive work environment.

5. Design and implementation of internal controls, such as:

   a. The appropriate level of oversight by those charged with governance of the company's assets, work methods, and employees.

   b. Segregation of duties relating to executing, recording, authorizing, and processing transactions.

   c. Restriction of access to assets and inventory stores to only authorized people, and implement appropriate security controls.

   d. Development of an effective information system that includes the functions by which transactions are initiated, recorded, processed, and transferred to account books and reported in financial statements.

   e. Physical controls, such as physical counting of inventory, investments, and other assets.

6. Management of the company should educate employees about the internal controls and how to perform the work correctly.

7. Management should hire only competent employees whose skills and attributes fit their job description and who do not have any known history of violations.

8. Internal audits can identify the deficiencies in internal controls, thereby helping to manage high-risk areas where the potential for fraud may exist. Internal audits also help in evaluating the effectiveness of the current control environment and identify areas for improvement.

9. A thorough and detailed investigation of all violations sends a strong message to potential violators.

10. Having a procedure manual is just another way of communicating with employees. This manual should clearly establish how tasks should be completed and suggest appropriate measures for prevailing circumstances.

Tools and Resources

1. Anti-Fraud Experts - http://www.acfe.com/ - Hire experts to help if you have a serious problem that you cannot solve by yourself.

2. Book: *Protect Your Business from Employee Fraud*, by Ali Asadi https://amzn.to/2L7xjyD

3. Book: *Wanted Employee Thieves: How a Forensic Fraud Examiner can save you time, money and stress by getting them to voluntarily confess...Internal Fraud Exposed*, by John Capizzi https://amzn.to/2zlEE8z

4. Book: *Preventing and Detecting Employee Theft and Embezzlement: A Practical Guide*, by Stephen Pedneault https://amzn.to/2Ht8xrX

5. Book: *Fraud 101: Techniques and Strategies for Understanding Fraud*, by Stephen Pedneault https://amzn.to/33WyFVE

How to Deal with Employee Theft and Fraud

Why is it Important?

Employee theft and fraud can start small, but if allowed to go unchecked, it can land you in serious trouble and can jeopardize the survival of your business. If one employee steals and is not checked, many others will see his example and be tempted to follow. The end result: losses of as much as 10 percent of your revenues.

Sometimes owners hesitate in taking corrective action in time. They may feel the need to retain key employees rather than pointing them out for theft. Once theft starts, however, it is only a time before it goes out of control and damages your business.

Fraud by employees can also involve you in legal issues with the government. The employee could be tampering with records to make some extra money for himself, but because your records or accounts are now incorrect, you could be held liable to legal action. The fact that some employees did this for personal gain will not protect you. The responsibility to submit correct accounts rests with you.

Quotes from Successful People

- *"Things gained through unjust fraud are never secure."* — **Sophocles**

- *"The first and worst of all frauds is to cheat one's self."* — **Philip James Bailey**

- *"The opposite of knowledge is not ignorance, but deceit and fraud."* — **Jean Baudrillard**

- *"For the most part fraud in the end secures for its companions repentance and shame."* — **Charles Simmons**

- *"But I'm acutely aware that the possibility of fraud is even more prevalent in today's world because of the Internet and cell phones and the opportunity for instant communication with strangers."* — **Armistead Maupin**

10 Great Tips

1. Managers should be aware of any conditions as well as behavioral red flags that suggest the possibility of fraudulent activities.

2. If fraud risk factors are present in the environment, management needs to set up a planned investigation for the detection of fraud and eliminate it from the root.

3. An internal audit, whistle-blowing policies, and strong internal controls are effective ways of discovering fraud.

4. Once fraud is detected, the very first action that the management of a company should take is stopping the fraud. Depending on how the fraud has been executed, management would restrict access to sources and employ more strict internal controls to prevent fraud in the future.

5. The second step involves the acquisition and verification of information related to the identified fraud. Depending on the nature of fraud and the suspected people involved, sources may vary.

6. After all, facts are collected; it is time to approach the person suspected of committing fraud. This discussion should be handled by personnel specializing in criminal activity and law, not by the auditors.

7. The discussion should move forward, depending on how the person responds. If he or she shows signs of ignorance or resistance, an intelligently designed inquiry should be conducted.

8. If fraud is established, the company should make the person aware that the offense will be reported to the police. Possible legal consequences should also be made clear and that the company will try to recover its assets and property through civil action.

9. The final step is to report the case to the local police or other independent agency. If the matter is left unreported, the company's reputation may be damaged. Moreover, the suspect may try to commit fraud in another business.

10. A detailed summary of events that led to fraud should be prepared that includes the conclusions drawn from the evidence obtained and the basis of allegations. This should also state how the investigation was carried out and the results obtained.

Tools and Resources

1. HG.org - https://www.hg.org/ - A great website full of all human resources laws and legal information.

2. Book: *Cyber Within: A Security Awareness Story and Guide for Employees (Cyber Crime & Fraud Prevention)*, by Christodonte II, Marcos https://amzn.to/2ME86Ps

3. Book: *Cybersecurity and Cyberwar: What Everyone Needs to Know*, by P. W. Singer and Allan Friedman https://amzn.to/2KVol3o

4. Book: *Cybersecurity Program Development for Business: The Essential Planning Guide*, by Chris Moschovitis https://amzn.to/2KVoJEu

5. Book: *Corporate Fraud Handbook: Prevention and Detection*, by Joseph T. Wells https://amzn.to/2KWabUX

Marketing & Advertising

How to Find the Best Tool to Market Your Business

Why is it Important?

The days when marketing your business was a simple affair are long gone. You may have the best product in the market, but if the intended customer does not know about it, your business will stagnate. There are, however, many ways that you can market your business and approach your clients. You must understand the options available to you and use them intelligently to take your message out to the maximum number of people at the lowest cost. If you look around, you will see that successful companies devote considerable time and effort to selecting the right tool to market their business.

Depending on the profile of your typical client, you will be required to select appropriate tools. For example, if your product is meant to be used by young mothers, you will need to select the media and design your message appropriately. If your end-user is not so clearly identifiable, however, you will need to segment your user groups and select the right tool, media, and message to connect with each of these segments individually. This alone will ensure that your marketing plan is effective and efficient. Modern communication technology has given you far more choices than ever before, but this requires business owners to be better prepared to take advantage of the technology available to them.

Quotes from Successful People

- *"Put your energy into making things that are likeable, not some douchey social media strategy."* — **Matthew Inman**

- *"You can't sell anything if you can't tell anything."* — **Beth Comstock**

- *"Don't be afraid to get creative and experiment with your marketing."* — **Mike Volpe**

- *"The best marketing doesn't feel like marketing."* — **Tom Fishburne**

- *"Marketing is no longer about the stuff that you make, but about the stories you tell."* — **Seth Godin**

10 Great Tips

1. Marketing is about building relationships, and advertising is only a part of marketing.

2. Keep in mind that marketing is like building a puzzle, so you need to get involved in different online and offline activities to create your image.

3. No marketing strategies will be successful without appropriate control measures to evaluate their effectiveness.

4. Your marketing effort has to be aligned with your business, and you have to keep fine-tuning it all the time.

5. Marketing efforts often suffer when business owners spend their time, energy, and money on unimportant tasks and unproductive processes.

6. Get feedback from both customers and employees about your current products and services and become aware of what customers want.

7. Develop a table including all your marketing activities, their expenses, and the number of leads or new customers that you get from each tool. Review this table every three months to see the most effective marketing tool.

8. Use a target group of customers as a sounding board for new ideas and products, which is often referred to as testing research.

9. Do not rely only on online activities. Go out and meet as many potential customers as you can.

10. Be patient! Consistency is the key to success. Sometimes it takes time to see the results of your marketing activities.

Tools and Resources

1. Buzzsumo - http://buzzsumo.com/ - Analyze what keywords and content work best for your business. With Buzzsumo, you can even analyze what is working for your competitors!

2. Hashtagify - https://hashtagify.me - Helps you identify the most successful and popular hashtags on social media in real-time. The results improve the success of your marketing efforts.

3. Google My Business - https://www.google.com/business/ - Most searches on Google are for local data, and Google's "My Business" lets you take full advantage of thousands of users in your vicinity who may be searching for a product you have to offer. Get great analytics, integration with Google Maps, and access your data from anywhere.

4. Hootsuite - https://hootsuite.com/ - Manage your entire social media effort from a single location. Multiply your productivity and connect better with your clients with this proven platform.

5. Followerwonk - https://moz.com/followerwonk/ - If Twitter is important to your marketing efforts, then this is one tool you must explore. It allows you to identify prospective clients and gives you prompts to identify the most effective time to post your tweets.

How to Evaluate Your Competitors

Why is it Important?

Before the Internet era, a small-business owner used to operate in a limited area and knew his market well. He had only a few competitors. In fact, if this small-business owner had a competitive advantage or a great product, his competition would be very limited. With e-commerce and global trade, however, this protection does not exist any longer. A competitor can emerge from anywhere in the world. Business people in today's environment have to be very vigilant and spend a lot more time understanding and studying the competition. They can only beat the competition when they understand the competitor well and offer clients higher quality service or products.

You must also study your competitors to understand their product range and the features of the products they offer. Much of this information is available freely as part of their marketing activities. This process also allows you to see how responsive your competitor is to an emailed request or query and how they interact with their customers and prospective clients. When you study your competitors this closely, you will be able to compare your procedures and products with theirs and be able to identify areas where you should improve.

Quotes from Successful People

- *"Be loyal to those who are loyal to you. And respect everyone, even your enemies and competition."* — **John Cena**

- *"Having no competition is a bad thing. Competition makes you try to improve yourself all the time."* — **Shu Qi**

- *"Becoming number one is easier than remaining number one."* — **Bill Bradley**

- *"Whenever I may be tempted to slack up and let the business run for a while on its own impetus, I picture my competitor sitting at a desk in his opposition house, thinking and thinking with the most devilish intensity and clearness, and I ask myself what I can do to be prepared for his next brilliant move."* — **H. Gordon Selfridge**

- *"Competition brings out the best in products and the worst in people."* — **David Sarnoff**

10 Great Tips

1. Understand who your competitors are. Are they more experienced than you are? Do they have an impressive list of clients?

2. Which of your competitors are doing better than you are? Why are they so good? How do they use technology, new distribution channels, and social media?

3. Have you asked your customers why they sometimes use competing products?

4. Have you studied your competitors to see their advertising campaigns, both online and offline?

5. Where are your competitors located geographically?

6. How does the competition price its goods or services?

7. What is the quality of customer service? How does it compare with yours?

8. Have you studied their staff and personnel management? How well is the staff paid and motivated?

9. How creative is the competition?

10. What is the financial strength of your competitors? How long have they been in business?

Tools and Resources

1. Google Alerts - https://www.google.com/alerts - Create an alert about your competitor or their products and get mail from Google every time there is a mention of it on the Internet. The service is free.

2. SocialMention - http://socialmention.com/ - A super easy-to-use tool that takes in a keyword or a phrase from you and gives you precise statistics and details about what social media has to say about your topic.

3. Monitor Backlinks - https://monitorbacklinks.com/home - Analyze why your competitors are getting great web traffic

and what is wrong with your websites. Use dashboards to improve your marketing efforts.

4. SEMrush - https://www.semrush.com/ - Give SEMrush the URL to a competitor's home page and get a whole lot of data regarding keyword, AdWords, and other information. Both free and paid versions exist.

5. SimilarWeb - https://www.similarweb.com/ - Hard-core marketing intelligence solutions. Enter your competitor's website and get a long list of detailed information about it. Once SimilarWeb understands who your competitors are, it will even suggest more businesses you may want to track.

How to Know More About Your Customers

Why is it Important?

No business can succeed if it does not understand its customers and their motivation behind purchasing. Even if you are selling something very basic, such as grocery items, you must remember that your customers have many different choices available to them. Why should they buy from you and not from someone else? The answer lies in understanding what is critical to individual customers. Some customers may value the speed of delivery; others may want to have a wide range of choices, while others may be looking only at price. Unless you know what is important to your customers, you will not be able to approach them most effectively.

With electronic databases and customer relationship management software, you now have the capability to maintain detailed records of every interaction you have had with every customer. If you use technology well, you should be able to predict the demands of your customers. It is pretty basic today to wish your clients on their important days and to send out a reminder to refill their monthly prescriptions. But can you go beyond this and surprise your clients with first-class, personalized service that will make them remember you the next time they need your product? This is only possible if you know your clients well.

Quotes from Successful People

- *"Your most unhappy customers are your greatest source of learning."* — **Bill Gates**

- *"Your customer doesn't care how much you know until they know how much you care."* — **Damon Richards**

- *"Know what your customers want most and what your company does best. Focus on where those two meet."* — **Kevin Stirtz**

- *"Make your product easier to buy than your competition, or you will find your customers buying from them, not you."* — **Mark Cuban**

- *"Here is a simple but powerful rule: always give people more than what they expect to get."* — **Nelson Boswell**

10 Great Tips

1. Analyzing your customers in the market helps build a bridge between market trends and customers. Every business is there to satisfy customers, but in order to be able to do that, it is vitally important to know who your customers are and what factors drive them to your business.

2. Who are your typical customers? (Do you actually have "typical" customers?) Can you classify them by age? Income? Gender? Locations?

3. Will your customers come straight to you, or will they do comparison shopping? How does your customer come to know about your product?

4. Why do your customers come to you? Why do they not go to anyone else? What is it about your product that your customers like, and what is it that they do not like?

5. Which of your 5 Ps do your customers like the most (product/pricing/placement/promotions/people)?

6. Is the quality of your product or service more important than price? What motivates your prospective customers to make a purchase?

7. Are the benefits the customer is looking for intangible or tangible? Which particular customer need does the product fulfill?

8. From where do your customers make a purchase? Are there different outlets? Are your customers' needs static? Or do they change over time?

9. How frequently do your customers purchase your product/services?

10. What quantities are purchased when customers buy your products?

Tools and Resources

1. Intercom - https://www.intercom.com - Intercom is a practical way of keeping in touch with your customers. It tracks every message you send your customers and gives you details about the best way to interact with them.

2. Kissmetrics - https://www.spacepencil.com/kissmetrics/ - Understand your customers' activity and requirements. Engage with them at a deeper level with detailed data about customer behavior.

3. Agile CRM - https://www.agilecrm.com/ - Get details of customer behavior with Agile CRM. Intuitive dashboards and very powerful features make this a tool of choice to understand customer patterns of behavior.

4. CloudCherry - https://www.getcloudcherry.com/ - This is a customer experience analytics tool that will unearth information you did not know you had. Every time a customer interacts with your company CloudCherry stores the interaction and adds to its database. The end result is actionable insights that add to your bottom line.

5. Brand24 - https://brand24.com/ - Know what your customers say about your brand and your products. Understand the conversations taking place, the influence score of customers, and the sentiments being expressed.

How to Find and Cooperate with Collaborators

Why is it Important?

Running an efficient and successful business requires owners/managers to work closely with many subsystem suppliers. Even if you are making the entire product completely in-house, it is unlikely that you will also be making the packing material and printing the product brochures in-house. Even though these may not seem so important, all of them are important to the final product. To put the entire product together successfully requires you to work closely with subcomponent and ancillary equipment suppliers. These collaborators are essential to the final success of your marketing effort.

With e-commerce and global supply chains, you can find the right supplier/collaborator in any part of the world. Some of these can be extremely efficient and innovative, and working with them can give you a great competitive advantage. Working with many different collaborators also allows you to diversify your subassembly procurement. This diversification covers you against many risks and ensures that your business will keep working even if one supplier is not able to give you the right supplies in time. You also need to understand that it is important to cooperate with your collaborators and build good working relationships. This will ensure that they will work extra hard for you and help you out if there is a difficult situation.

Quotes from Successful People

- *"Teamwork begins by building trust. And the only way to do that is to overcome our need for invulnerability."* — **Patrick Lencioni**

- *"If you want to lift yourself up, lift up someone else."* — **Booker T. Washington**

- *"No one can whistle a symphony. It takes a whole orchestra to play it."* — **H.E. Luccock**

- *"Effectively, change is almost impossible without industry-wide collaboration, cooperation, and consensus."* — **Simon Mainwaring**

- *"No matter how brilliant your mind or strategy, if you're playing a solo game, you'll always lose out to a team."* — **Reid Hoffman**

10 Great Tips

1. You must consider making a good relationship with some other businesses or companies that are related to your business but are not your competitors.

2. Payment gateways, banks, transport companies, and governmental or technical companies that you deal with could all be identified as potential collaborators.

3. Are you outsourcing any activities? To whom? Where? And how are your working relationships?

4. What channels of collaboration do you use? Who are your prime collaborators?

5. How do you choose your collaborators? How do they choose you?

6. How does your product relate to your collaborators' business?

7. How do your collaborators make decisions about their relationships? What influences their decisions?

8. How important is your product/service to your collaborators?

9. What do your collaborators need from you? Are your collaborators closely aligned with you, or is it just a buyer/seller relationship?

10. What does your collaborator network consist of? Do you know enough about its

   a. Type

   b. Size

   c. Geographical regions

   d. Markets

Tools and Resources

1. Flock - https://flock.com - Improve communication with business collaborators and build teams that can work on different projects simultaneously. Flock supports many different modes of communication in a securely encrypted format.

2. Workplace by Facebook - https://www.facebook.com/workplace/ - Hold conversations with your business collaborators and share data, files, and videos with ease. Get real-time responses and work across the globe with in-built translators.

3. Book: *Supplier Relationship Management A Complete Guide*, by Gerardus Blokdyk https://amzn.to/2KYMqvH

4. Book: *The Vendor Management Office: Unleashing the Power of Strategic Sourcing*, by Stephen Gut https://amzn.to/2KUJsbs

5. Book: *Mastering Collaboration: Make Working Together Less Painful and More Productive*, by Gretchen Anderson https://amzn.to/2KVcuaM

How to Analyze the Market Situation

Why is it Important?

Your marketing efforts will only succeed if you have done a very good analysis of your market. This analysis gives you a scientific approach to answering basic questions that affect your business. These questions cover the following:

- Information about customers

- Understanding the marketing landscape and competitors

- The market risks the business faces

- The brand value of your business

With structured market analysis, you no longer have to run your business based on guesswork or intuition. You have a good action plan that is based on sound research.

Market analysis also makes you focus on the customer. It makes you understand why exactly the customer is buying your product. Once this is clear, you can focus on finding other customers with similar needs. Market research will also give you information about new trends and technologies that affect your business. The analysis will also give you inputs about any regulations that may be changing or likely to change in the future. This information will help you prepare better for the changes that you need to handle.

Market situation analysis also helps you identify risks to your business and take timely corrective action. This ensures that you maintain and grow your market share and profitability.

Quotes from Successful People

- *"The price of light is less than the cost of darkness."* — **Arthur C. Nielsen**

- *"War is ninety percent information."* — **Napoleon Bonaparte**

- *"I never guess. It is a capital mistake to theorize before one has data. Insensibly one begins to twist facts to suit theories, instead of theories to suit facts."* — **Sir Arthur Conan Doyle**

- *"If you torture the data long enough, it will confess."* — **Ronald Coase**

- *"Data are just summaries of thousands of stories—tell a few of those stories to help make the data meaningful."* — **Chip & Dan Heath**

10 Great Tips

1. The climate of your market and the forces of supply and demand have a profound effect on the way your business performs.

2. Conducting a market analysis involves the assessment of your target population and the need for your product in the market you want to target.

3. What market are you trying to reach? This could be geographic or demographic, depending on your target audience.

4. What is the size of this market?

5. Is the market volatile, stable, or growing?

6. How has this market treated previous players? Have they been successful? If so, what is the business model that has helped them attract this market? What about the ones that failed? Why did they fail?

7. Is that market likely to be influenced by political or economic decisions in the future? Are there likely to be trade laws or business regulations that might hinder business growth?

8. Is the market saturated or wide open? Is there space for a new player?

9. You can conduct an effective analysis of market climate by choosing either primary research (which you can do yourself)

or secondary research (where you can refer to previous analysis).

10. PEST analysis is one of the best tools to scan the macroenvironmental factors that affect your business. The acronym PEST stands for political, environmental, social, and technological analysis.

Tools and Resources

1. Think with Google - https://www.thinkwithgoogle.com/ - Think with Google gives you free tools to conduct in-depth market analysis. Gauge citywide trends, know what people look for, how your website performs, and more.

2. American Fact Finder - https://factfinder.census.gov - A great tool to research the U.S. population. This tool is based on the U.S. census and gives you answers to different questions and surveys. Get to know your target customers better with this free tool.

3. Claritas - https://www.claritas.com/ - Understand your market and its various segments. Use this information to create actionable plans and insights.

4. Temper - https://www.temper.io/ - Temper can measure and give you a graphical representation of how your customers and partners feel about a certain product or feature. Measuring market reaction to your product will put you on the path to improving your product.

5. Pew Research Center - http://www.pewresearch.org/download-datasets/ - Get ready access to Pew Research Center datasets about the U.S. market for free. Use the information to improve your market analysis and fine-tune your growth plans.

How to Spend Your Marketing Budget Wisely

Why is it Important?

Small businesses operate on budgets that need to be prioritized very carefully. Many important business needs compete for the same budget. If you have a limited amount to spend on your marketing activities, you must make sure that this is spent well and gives you the best return on your money.

It is important to understand your typical customer and their priorities. Once you find out who your customers are and what appeals to them, you can plan your marketing methods and expenditure. A good marketing plan will ensure that the correct group of people are approached and helps you find the best tools to target your potential customers effectively and efficiently.

Do not rush into spending your marketing funds into new fads. Social media is important, but think whether you really want to target people in different countries or should you focus on your local markets. This clarity will help you build a business on a solid foundation and grow solidly rather than spreading yourself too thin.

Quotes from Successful People

- *"The budget is not just a collection of numbers, but an expression of our values and aspirations."* — **Jacob Lew**

- *"Nobody counts the number of ads you run; they just remember the impression you make."* — **Bill Bernbach**

- *"Stopping advertising to save money is like stopping your watch to save time."* — **Henry Ford**

- *"Don't tell me how good you make it; tell me how good it makes me when I use it."* — **Leo Burnett**

- *"Make it simple. Make it memorable. Make it inviting to look at."* — **Leo Burnett**

10 Great Tips

1. Budgeting for your strategic marketing plan must ensure that your marketing strategies are realistically priced.

2. You'd typically have to dig deeper to decide where your hard-earned dollars are best spent, and resources are most effective.

3. Marketing gurus recommend that established businesses spend anywhere from 1 percent to 10 percent of previous sales on marketing.

4. New businesses might want to spend a little more (even up to 15 percent), as they have to work on getting their product known to prospective customers.

5. Take care to leverage free and low-cost marketing tools, such as social media.

6. You will need to use every possible method and communication channel to make your target customer group aware of what you have to offer and how it is special.

7. Keep a watch on how much your competitors are spending.

8. Track your budget regularly to keep it on target. Determine how much you have spent in one week on your marketing plan and how many customers have made purchases.

9. Avoid budgeting yourself into a corner. Keep some breathing space, especially with an economy lurking in the background.

10. Assign budgets for both online and offline marketing activities. Make a list of all your marketing tools and channels and review their effectiveness

Tools and Resources

1. HubSpot - https://blog.hubspot.com/marketing - Use the many free resources given at this website to understand where your marketing dollars are going and how you can spend your budget better.

2. Marketing Donut - https://www.marketingdonut.co.uk/ - If you are unsure about creating your marketing plan and want to work using proven templates that have done part of the hard work already, then this is a good resource to start from.

3. Book: *The Golden Rules of Practical Marketing: What Every Business Owner Must Know*, by Ali Asadi
https://amzn.to/324aNO8

4. Book: *Outrageous Marketing: The Story of The Onion and How to Build a Powerful Brand with No Marketing Budget*, by Scott Dikkers https://amzn.to/3236L8B

5. Book: *The 1-Page Marketing Plan: Get New Customers, Make More Money, And Stand out From The Crowd*, by Allan Dib
https://amzn.to/326g1sF

How to Have a Perfect Business Card

Why is it Important?

As for marketing your brand, having a great business card handy at all times is a smart way to begin. Even though almost everything concerned with running your business may have gone digital, the business card is still around.

A quality card ensures you come across as serious about your work and makes a great first impression. It stays with the person you hand it to and can be a good introduction to your brand. By giving out your card, you are able to share your phone numbers, fax, websites, and emails all at one go. This saves time and prevents any spelling mistakes or errors.

Carrying a good-quality business card with you also indicates that you are prepared to run your business efficiently and will not let any opportunity pass. Besides, if you take the trouble to embed your card with electronic data and innovative materials and design, your card will not be thrown away. It will be passed around. This is exactly what you want.

Quotes from Successful People

- *"Making a strong first impression is as important as ever, especially when meeting face-to-face."* — **Joseph Abboud**

- *"Design is how you make your first impression with your consumers. Make sure it is a lasting one."* — **Jay Samit**

- *"Our work is the presentation of our capabilities."* — **Edward Gibbon**

- *"Details create the big picture."* — **Sanford I. Weill**

- *"My belief is you have one chance to make a first impression."* — **Kevin McCarthy**

10 Great Tips

1. A business card is probably the first impression of your business when you meet new people, so it is very important to have a professional one.

2. Make it simple. You do not need to put all the information about your business on your business card

3. Use standard sizes.

4. The number of colors you use in designs depends on the type of your profession.

5. Brand it with a slogan. As an example, one of my slogans is "One Idea Can Change Your Business Forever."

6. Ask a professional designer to design your card and use high-quality paper for printing.

7. Full name, title, phone number, email address, office address, and website are the main elements of every business card.

8. Never leave your house without your business cards. You never know when you may face business opportunities.

9. Give people more than two cards so they can give them to others.

10. It is recommended that your business card designs and colors be compatible with your website, banners, and flyers to make branding stronger.

Tools and Resources

1. Business Card Land - http://www.businesscardland.com/home/ - If you just want to create a simple and straightforward business card, then Business Card Land is the right place to come to. You can choose from a number of different templates and standard sizes.

2. Gotprint - https://www.gotprint.com - Design and publish your cards with ease. Select from a wide variety of templates and designs. Print yourself or get them delivered to you.

3. Biz Card Creator - https://bizcardcreator.com/ - Create and print business cards in a jiffy. Use any of the large collections of templates, artwork, and fonts. This tool is absolutely free.

4. Degraeve - http://www.degraeve.com/business-cards - Get high-quality business cards and also design your company logo. Get a pdf file that can be sent to a local printer or even be printed at home.

5. Zazzle - https://www.zazzle.com/businesscards - A single-point solution to design very high-quality business cards and get them printed and shipped to you within 24 hours.

How to Create Great Brochures and Flyers

Why is it Important?

When you meet prospective clients at a trade event or other similar occasions, you will not be able to get much of their time. After all, the person is strolling around and has hundreds of other distractions competing for their attention. If you can arouse this person's curiosity, however, and get them interested enough to take one of your brochures or flyers, chances are they will look it over when they have more time.

You need to put in thought and careful design into your brochure or flyer. Too many people make the mistake of stuffing it with information. This makes the brochure look complex and unattractive. Well-designed brochures focus on a single activity. They describe one aspect of your business and do it well. This is why you may have seen businesses create many different versions of brochures. Each deals with one aspect of their work.

In many ways, the brochure supports your website and caters to the prospect who shows interest but does not have the inclination to go to the web to check you out. The brochure is perfect for such people.

A well-designed brochure will persuade the reader to perform a specific action. Perhaps it is to make the reader interested enough to give you a call or drop an email. Perhaps you can make the reader ask you for a sample or a quote. If the reader takes any action in response to the flyer, you know they have moved one step further toward making a purchase decision.

Quotes from Successful People

- *"There are three responses to a piece of design—yes, no, and WOW! Wow is the one to aim for."* — **Milton Glaser**

- *"Socrates said, 'Know thyself.' I say, 'Know thy users.' And guess what? They don't think like you do."* — **Joshua Brewer**

- *"I strive for two things in design: simplicity and clarity. Great design is born of those two things."* — **Lindon Leader**

- *"Content precedes design. Design in the absence of content is not design, it's decoration."* — **Jeffrey Zeldman**

- *"Creativity is just connecting things. When you ask creative people how they did something, they feel a little guilty because they didn't really do it, they just saw something. It seemed obvious to them after a while."* — **Steve Jobs**

10 Great Tips

1. A brochure serves as an important introductory document for any business.

2. Brochures offer a professional and effective platform to present valuable information free of cost to your customers.

3. First, settle your brochure size before starting anything else. Too many people waste effort by trying to refit everything later.

4. Work to an overall concept and theme so that everything looks matched and cohesive. Ensure your photos and illustrations are of high quality and that the colors print well.

5. Use fonts and sizes imaginatively but with some sophistication so that the overall effort suits the product.

6. Use bullets, headlines, tables, charts, and illustrations to deliver your message effectively. Remember that people absorb information differently. Your brochure must cater to as many of them as possible.

7. Ensure there is a call to action—ask your readers to visit your website, showroom, or send an email query or call. The aim of the brochure is to get the reader to do something

8. Go for quality—great content, great paper, and great printing. Your aim is to ensure that readers find your brochure so good that they are reluctant to throw it away.

9. Brochures can be designed online in a wide variety of aesthetic formats to suit your unique requirements and budgets.

10. Do not make your brochure too busy and confusing, with too much information.

Tools and Resources

1. Canva - https://www.canva.com/ - A professional brochure designing tool that can get you classy brochures in no time at all.

2. Edraw Brochure - https://www.edrawsoft.com/ - Work on a blank page or start from a well-designed template. Either way, you get your brochures done fast.

3. Lucidpress Online Brochures - https://www.lucidpress.com/ - Work from a large number of templates and designs to impress your customers and audience.

4. Adobe Spark - https://spark.adobe.com/ - Get set on your creative journey with Adobe Spark! There is no end to the things you can achieve with this proven tool.

5. SmartDraw - https://www.smartdraw.com/ - SmartDraw comes in two versions—an online version where you just connect and start your work or a downloadable version you can install on your Windows PC. Either way, you get great results.

How to Use Facebook for Your Business

Why is it Important?

Many owners of small businesses may think Facebook is just to stay connected with people. They are wrong. Facebook can be a solid business tool and can give them a head start over their competition. You must put in the effort to understand Facebook and to use it to market your business better.

FB allows you to collect leads in the form of email IDs and phone numbers of people who show an interest in your business and what it offers. This allows you to contact them outside Facebook and send them relevant information.

It costs you nothing to set up a Facebook business page. You can do it yourself and need not hire an expert. The structure is there, and customizing it to your look and feel is easy. Many clients look for authenticity and feedback from real users of your product. You can reach a targeted audience by designing ads that are shown only to people who match the criterion you define. This gives you far more value for your money as compared with an ad that is sprayed across to everyone.

Facebook also offers great analytics and insights. You don't need an advanced degree in math to understand the data your pages generate. If you follow the insights Facebook provides, you have the potential to take your marketing efforts to a higher plane.

Quotes from Successful People

- *"Facebook was not originally created to be a company. It was built to accomplish a social mission—to make the world more open and connected." —* **Mark Zuckerberg**

- *"Think about what people are doing on Facebook today. They're keeping up with their friends and family, but they're also building an image and identity for themselves, which in a sense is their brand. They're connecting with the audience that they want to connect to. It's almost a disadvantage if you're not on it now." —* **Mark Zuckerberg**

- *"Once I found this possibility to use Twitter and Facebook and my blog to connect to my readers, I'm going to use it, to connect to them and to share thoughts that I cannot use in the book."* — **Paulo Coelho**

- *"The Facebook way is that you sit at the table and you state your opinion, back it up with data, and make a recommendation."* — **Marne Levine**

- *"Social networking websites like Facebook, Twitter, and Tumblr provide an unparalleled ability for people to stay connected in new and unique ways."* — **Michael Bennet**

10 Great Tips

1. Provide information about your business—your profile on Facebook is the first introduction many prospective customers will have about your business and what it stands for. Make sure that your profile is well built and gives an impression of integrity, professionalism, and elegance.

2. Build some excitement and buzz—avoid boring your readers. Ten seconds is all you get to help them make up their minds.

3. Analyze your target audience and focus on them—do not try to target all people on Facebook. Write for those who are likely to be interested in your product and may search for it.

4. Let your prospective customers get a real feel of the benefits of doing business with you. Use testimonials and reviews to great effect.

5. Choose a great URL—this is the address of your Facebook page. Instead of Facebook.com/tom1985, see if you can get Facebook.com/great_kitchen_gardens if that is your line of business.

6. Use pictures with care, imagination, and style. A picture is worth a thousand words—but only if it is chosen well.

7. Build a network—visit others' pages and leave professional comments. Build a presence of like-minded people.

8. Use your Facebook page to interact with your customers and react to their comments and complaints. React promptly to both, and you will generate a lot of goodwill.

9. Post regularly on your Facebook page. This will keep your page active and help it show up more easily in searches.

10. Keep your customers interested by running contests and polls. Give out rewards and coupons to keep users coming back.

Tools and Resources

1. DriftRock - https://www.driftrock.com/ - Unlock the value in your customer data by using this great Facebook tool. Reduce expenditures on ads and improve your results.

2. Likealyzer - https://likealyzer.com/ - A Facebook advisor that works for you to optimize your Facebook campaigns. Get instant comparisons with competitors to know how your campaign compares.

3. ShortStack - https://www.shortstack.com/facebook/ - Simplifies the creation of ads on the Facebook Platform. Works on many other social media sites as well to give you a complete advertising solution.

4. Social Bakers - https://www.socialbakers.com/ - Uses Artificial Intelligence to analyze your Facebook marketing efforts and improve their results.

5. Book: *Social Media Marketing Workbook: How to Use Social Media for Business*, by Jason McDonald https://amzn.to/3229Upg

How to Use LinkedIn for Your Business

Why is it Important?

Many people are not aware that LinkedIn is not just for individuals. You can have a company page on LinkedIn as well. There are many benefits of having a company page, and LinkedIn gives you many additional features and information if you have a company page on their site. These analytical tools give you information about how many times your company page was viewed, and the number of clicks your posts generated.

On your company page, you can share important news about your company. You can place the really important information right at the top of the page and can pin it there to ensure that it doesn't shift even if new posts are added.

You are automatically notified if any LinkedIn users mention the name of your company on their page. This helps you stay updated with what people say about you. Your employees can add your company to the experience section of their profile. This creates a link back to your company page. Smart business owners take advantage of LinkedIn to get wider exposure and use their employees to create links to their company, thereby increasing the possibilities of reaching much larger numbers of people.

Quotes from Successful People

- *"Active participation on LinkedIn is the best way to say, 'Look at me!' without saying 'Look at me!"* — **Bobby Darnell**

- *"A huge number of jobs that are filled are never advertised to the public, or if they are, they're filled by people who have a connection to the employer."* — **Melanie Pinola**

- *"Your LinkedIn profile must be consistent with how you portray yourself elsewhere. Not only should your official résumé match the experience you list on LinkedIn, but it also should be consistent with Twitter and public Facebook information."* — **Melanie Pinola**

- *"Facebook asks me what's on my mind. Twitter asks me what's going on. LinkedIn wants me to reconnect with my colleagues. And YouTube tells me what to watch. Social Media is no reality show or Big Brother. It's but a smothering mother!"* — **Ana Claudia Antunes**

- *"One of the great things about LinkedIn is it isn't the same kind of networking that happens at conventions, where you're wearing a name tag, trying to meet strangers, and awkwardly attempting to make small talk. LinkedIn is networking without the pressure."* — **Melanie Pinola**

10 Great Tips

1. LinkedIn is a solid business and highly regarded in the business world. While many people use LinkedIn for professional networking, you can use it to connect with customers, hire new employees, and make successful business partnerships.

2. Use LinkedIn to obtain testimonials and referrals from previous clients to attract others who might be interested in the service as well.

3. Join groups that discuss the line of business you are in, or you could start one of your own. These professional groups help you get established as someone who knows.

4. Create a great public profile. Add professional background and headshot photos.

5. Choose your title wisely and add effective keywords to be found easily.

6. Create a page for your company and add your work samples to your profile.

7. Add your professional skills to get endorsed by your connections.

8. Link your LinkedIn profile to your website and other social networks.

9. Post business updates, videos, slides, and articles regularly and share them with LinkedIn groups you joined.

10. Write comments and ask questions from other professionals.

Tools and Resources

1. Crystal - https://www.crystalknows.com/ - Often called the largest personality program in the world, Crystal helps you analyze LinkedIn users and tailor your messages to them specifically.

2. Dux-Soup - https://www.dux-soup.com/ - If you visit a lot of LinkedIn profiles, use Dux-Soup to track them automatically. You only need to visit a page once, and Dux-Soup will build a database with all the essential details.

3. eLink Pro - https://elink-pro.com/ - Makes it easy to connect with large numbers of people on LinkedIn simultaneously. Just specify your criteria, and eLink Pro will find out all the relevant people automatically.

4. IFTTT - https://ifttt.com/linkedin - If This – Then That – is a great tool for sharing content on LinkedIn with the least amount of effort. Get notified automatically if a specified event occurs on LinkedIn.

5. LeadFuze - https://www.leadfuze.com/ - Completely automates the process of finding leads on LinkedIn. It also has built-in email and follow-up features.

How to Use Instagram for Your Business

Why is it Important?

In many cases, businesses miss out on promoting themselves in a visual manner that appeals to their target audience. Instagram is the perfect medium for visual storytelling. It allows you to engage closely with your customers and create emotional bonding with them.

Instagram has become a very large platform over the years. If you have tried to learn the correct way to use hashtags on Instagram, you will be able to make your product and service stand out and will connect directly with those who are looking for what you can deliver.

While interacting with users on Instagram, you will get a lot of feedback and insights from people. You can use this information to improve your product and build strong links with your audience. These links help your marketing efforts. Learning to use Instagram well is one investment that will pay you rich dividends.

Quotes from Successful People

- *"Instagram is my edit of my life."* — **Kendall Jenner**

- *"In the past, people have looked at photos as a record of memory. The focus has been on the past tense. With Instagram, the focus is on the present tense."* — **Kevin Systrom**

- *"Instagram has a faster chance of reaching me than CNN, and if I really want to know what's going on, I refresh my Twitter feed."* — **Emily Weiss**

- *"When you're doing a startup, life is not all roses and rainbows, like you see on Instagram, and killing it."* — **Paige Craig**

- *"Instagram has become one of my favorite platforms because of its simplicity."* — **Amy Jo Martin**

10 Great Tips

1. Instagram is one of the most important branding tools that can be helpful for various types of businesses. By using Instagram, you can share images or videos regarding your products or services with a lot of people.

2. Get great ideas by following top businesses in your industry and also check out your competitors on Instagram

3. Try to post at least three times a day. The time of posting depends on your followers. Test posts at different times to see what time gets the most attention.

4. Write an effective bio (150 characters) about your business and products or services you provide. You should also use

hashtags with related keywords to teach your followers the main areas of your activities.

5. If you use Instagram for your business, your image could be your logo or a professional photo of yourself.

6. Follow influencers in your industry, write comments on people's posts, and connect with them.

7. Connect Instagram to your other social networks, and add the Instagram icon to your website.

8. Instagram allows users to use thirty hashtags, but try not to use too many hashtags. It is much better to have solid followers than too many followers with various unrelated backgrounds.

9. Use image applications to post more attractive images on Instagram.

10. Write short descriptions about your posts, and encourage your followers to write comments and share your posts.

Tools and Resources

1. Buffer - https://buffer.com/ - Use Buffer to manage your Instagram campaign, get in-depth analytics, and schedule your posts to ensure you always have new content on your pages.

2. Sendible - https://www.sendible.com/?afmc=25 - Schedule your Instagram updates, interact with your followers, and collaborate with your team to build a great social media presence.

3. Later - https://later.com/ - Use Later to plan your Instagram activity in advance in just a few minutes of work. Manage a number of social media profiles simultaneously from simple, easy-to-use dashboards.

4. Iconosquare - https://pro.iconosquare.com/ - Unlock the potential of Instagram using Iconosquare. Use Instagram and Facebook together to get even better results than by using any platform by itself.

5. Social Insights - https://socialinsight.io/ - Monitor your growth using proven Instagram analytics. It shows you the best time to post, give you more than 28 analytical inputs, and manage many accounts from a common interface.

How to Use Pinterest for Your Business

Why is it Important?

If you are looking to market your business better, Pinterest is one platform you cannot afford to miss. Business owners often think that Pinterest is just a social media tool that has no real business use, but they are wrong. Pinterest is ideally suited to create purchasing intent in prospective clients. If you use it well, you will see a measurable increase in sales.

Since Pinterest has such a strong presence in the online world, businesses that use it actively find themselves ranking higher on search engines, getting more traffic, and reach a much wider audience.

Pinterest has also taken several steps to make itself of greater use to businesses. It has also created several tools to do this. For example, Rich Pins allow you to embed real-time pricing information and other details, and people who have pinned you can be sent direct notifications in case of a price reduction. All of these and other tools make Pinterest a great tool to use in your marketing efforts.

Quotes from Successful People

- *"You are what you share."* — **Charles W. Leadbeater**

- *"Social media spark a revelation that we, the people, have a voice, and through the democratization of content and ideas we can once again unite around common passions, inspire movements, and ignite change."* — **Brian Solis**

- *"The more passionate and argumentative I get the more followers and friends I make online."* — **Tasha Turner**

- *"I'm not addicted to the social networks. I only use them anytime I've got time for it . . . break time, brunch time, lunch time, party time, bedtime, anytime and every time."* — **Ifeoluwa Egbetade**

- *"If Content is king and Context is queen, then Conversation is the kingdom and Contact information is the currency."* — **Abraham Varghese**

10 Great Tips

1. Considered to be one of the fastest-growing social media sites in the world.

2. When you become a member of Pinterest (for free), you create your pinboard. On this board, you can pin pages, pictures, videos, and other kinds of media files you like on other websites.

3. Add keywords to your boards so that people can easily find your boards.

4. Use keywords in your descriptions and make your descriptions short so that people can tweet your post as well.

5. Follow top influencers in your industry to see how they promote themselves through Pinterest.

6. Use hashtags in your descriptions to be found by people. Add your website URL to the description.

7. Link your Pinterest profile to your website and other social networks.

8. Use Pinterest for business accounts to be able to access your profile analytics.

9. Develop collaborative boards so that other Pinterest users can share their posts on your board. This can improve your profile visibility and the number of your followers.

10. Use Pinterest tools, such as Rich Pins and embed pins, and post different types of content, including YouTube videos, articles, audio links, and slides to get the most out of Pinterest

Tools and Resources

1. Buffer - https://buffer.com/pinterest - Schedule your pins and pin from any website you like. Measure the performance of your Pinterest activity and optimize your activity with very little effort.

2. Tailwind - https://www.tailwindapp.com - Get going with visual marketing to capture your market with ease. Schedule posts, discover content, and analyze your effort all in one neat package.

3. Viraltag - https://www.viraltag.com/ - Work with the entire spectrum of visual marketing applications with a strong focus on Pinterest. Build and maintain very close engagement with your audience to push the efficiency of your marketing efforts.

4. Viralwoot - https://viralwoot.com/ - Some tools allow you to schedule pins. This one gives you social media analytics, influencer engagement, and a content manager as well.

5. Smartly - https://www.smartly.io - A great tool to create visual ads.

How to Use Twitter for Your Business

Why is it Important?

Businesses have learned that Twitter is a perfect tool to market themselves effectively in today's fast-moving, ever-changing world. Smart businesses use Twitter to create a buzz about their products and activities and respond rapidly to customer feedback and queries.

Twitter allows you to segment your target audience and create detailed advertising campaigns that target just the right people. This gives you the best possible return on the time and effort you have invested. In addition, Twitter also lets you gain a good understanding of what people are saying about your product and your business. This information, if used well, makes your business more responsive to customer feedback. Using Twitter, you can get to know what customers do not like about your product or service and can take corrective action very rapidly.

While using Twitter is a great way to market your business, you need to do it professionally to ensure you do not spam your audience. A well-run Twitter campaign is informative, entertaining, and rewarding.

Quotes from Successful People

- *"Whatever one thinks of Twitter, the Friday Reads hashtag is kind of a cool tradition."* — **James Bernard Frost**

- *"Twitter is my bar. I sit at the counter and listen to the conversations, starting others, feeling the atmosphere."* — **Paulo Coelho**

- *"The use of the Internet, the use of Twitter, the way protest movements developed . . . This is a different world."* — **Gus O'Donnell**

- *"Twitter and Facebook are such amazing networks for me to introduce myself to the world and for fans around the world to introduce themselves to me."* — **Jenn Proske**

- *"I think Twitter is the future of communications and Square will be the payment network."* — **Jack Dorsey**

10 Great Tips

1. Twitter is a very popular microblogging service that is used by a great many professional people to keep their audience informed and updated about current events in their field of interest.

2. Each tweet is like a small text message—no longer than 140 characters. The message goes out to everyone who has signed on to "follow" you. As you have more followers, more people will read your messages.

3. If you can make your tweets interesting and useful, your readers will retweet them to others who are also interested in the same thing. This enhances your brand value immensely and introduces you to new prospects.

4. Find successful people in your industry and related fields, connect with them, and retweet their posts.

5. Do not use more than three hashtags in your tweet since it will decrease its effectiveness.

6. Use proper profile and background images for your Twitter account.

7. Monitor keyword searches by people to get a lot of information about new trends in your industry.

8. Provide business-related content. Do not send personal information through your business account.

9. Link your Twitter account to other social networks, such as Facebook, LinkedIn, and Instagram.

10. Do not tweet more than six or fewer than two times per day. Be patient. It takes time to get a lot of followers and attention through social networks, especially Twitter.

Tools and Resources

1. Rite Tag - https://ritetag.com/ - Selecting the right hashtag for your Twitter campaign is extremely important. Rite Tag ensures you get it right the first time. No wasted tweets and no wasted time.

2. TrendsMap - https://www.trendsmap.com/ - See global Twitter trends maps to instantly know what is important in the locations you are interested in. Zoom in to the level of detail you want.

3. Sprout Social - https://sproutsocial.com - A complete social media management platform that comes with great tools built especially for Twitter users. If you have several different Twitter campaigns going on, Sprout Social will help you keep track of them all.

4. BuzzSumo - http://buzzsumo.com/ - Typically, you want to use Twitter to drive users to your website. Are you successful? BuzzSumo will tell you that and give you a whole lot of additional statistics about how your Twitter activities are doing.

5. Twitonomy - https://www.twitonomy.com/ - A free tool to analyze tweets and get insights for your marketing activities.

How to Use YouTube for Your Business

Why is it Important?

One has to marvel at the insights of the founders who set up YouTube. What appeared to be just an entertainment platform has evolved very rapidly into a business tool that has no equal. Businesses can use YouTube for several key purposes. Some of the more important ones are discussed below.

YouTube helps your marketing effort by explaining your product and its advantages in the most professional way possible. A well-produced video can show your customers how your product will meet their requirements. Even if your product is still under development, you can use YouTube to show clients what to expect and can get valuable feedback that will help you refine your product and meet customer expectations better.

You can use the YouTube insight feature to get statistical reports on which of your videos are more popular, the kind of people who see them, and what their comments are. This allows you to alter your marketing plans in real-time and get the best from your marketing efforts.

Quotes from Successful People

- *"I think one of the most beautiful things about YouTube is that it makes the world a smaller place. You realize that we're all different, but we're all the same. And if you think about it, it's a beautiful concept."* — **Lilly Singh**

- *"YouTube is becoming much more than an entertainment destination."* — **Chad Hurley**

- *"The thing that has made YouTube so successful is that you can relate to the people you're watching to a much higher degree than to the people you see on TV."* — **PewDiePie**

- *"My journey began when I found out about YouTube on how do you make music, and from that, people started explaining me how I had to do it."* — **Alan Walker**

- *"I really grew my own fan base. I started posting videos on YouTube with the help of my parents."* — **Tori Kelly**

10 Great Tips

1. Create a professional YouTube channel with a background image, a short description, and linking other social networks and your website.

2. Choose great titles for your videos.

3. Add a well-written description and choose proper tags and category for each video.

4. Add a call to action to your videos.

5. Post your YouTube videos on all social networks.

6. Encourage people to subscribe to your YouTube channel.

7. Create playlists, including related videos.

8. Make a short introductory video about your business and put it on your channel.

9. Let your visitors add comments and talk about your videos.

10. Use YouTube analytical tools to get useful information about your viewers and analyze the effectiveness of your videos.

Tools and Resources

1. Keyword Tools - https://keywordtool.io/youtube - Use the YouTube autocomplete feature to generate relevant keywords for your videos. Learn what customers value and tailor your videos accordingly.

2. DrumUp - https://drumup.io/ - Cut your social media management time by 90 percent by using Drum Up to share your videos across different channels.

3. VidIQ - https://vidiq.com/ - Increase the library of your tags by ten times by using VidIQ. This immediately translates into much greater views for your videos. Build better brand awareness and recall.

4. Cyfe - https://www.cyfe.com/ - Get a dashboard that can analyze your social media campaigns and give you quality inputs to get your videos on their way to becoming viral.

5. Agorapulse - https://www.agorapulse.com/ - A social media management tool that is so effective for YouTube marketing.

How to Effectively Use Your Customers Testimonials

Why is it Important?

Customers value the information that is provided by other users of your product. Input from real users are convincing and assure other customers that what you say is not mere marketing hype but has been confirmed by independent sources. This is the value of customer testimonials.

You can collect customer testimonials from your product pages, your blogs, and emails that customers send you. In case you have solved a tough problem for a particular customer, you can request them for a testimonial as well.

Customer testimonials can be displayed in several places where they are likely to catch the attention of other customers and visitors. You can put them on your website, blogs, sales material, mailers, and other matters that you share with customers.

Testimonials need not be written down alone. You can also get a video testimonial that you can post on YouTube or your website. Video is often better than a written testimonial because a real customer on video using your product is more authentic.

Credibility is an essential requirement for the success of your business, and customer testimonials are a proven way of giving confidence to prospective clients.

Quotes from Successful People

- *"A satisfied customer is one who will continue to buy from you, seldom shop around, refer other customers and in general be a superstar advocate for your business."* — **Gregory Ciotti**

- *"Loyal customers, they don't just come back, they don't simply recommend you, they insist that their friends do business with you."* — **Chip Bell**

- *"Customer service shouldn't just be a department, it should be the entire company."* — **Tony Hsieh**

- *"If you make a sale, you can make a living. If you make an investment of time and good service in a customer, you can make a fortune."* — **Jim Rohn**

- *"The first step in exceeding your customer's expectations is to know those expectations."* — **Roy H. Williams**

10 Great Tips

1. You must select your best clients and especially choose those who have something very special to say about your work.

2. The testimonial must go beyond saying that your product/service is very good. It must highlight specific features or capabilities.

3. The entire idea behind the testimonial is to ensure that they help prospective clients decide that your business is right for them. You will need to review the testimonials periodically as your business evolves.

4. Never link testimonials with a reward or a prize. The comment must be genuine and given freely.

5. Tell your customers that you are seeking their testimonials on several different websites. Yelp.com, Google Place, Bing Place for business, Yahoo Local, Local.com, MerchantCircle, and Angieslist.com are some prominent ones.

6. Testimonials on your website are very useful too.

7. Increase the credibility of the testimonial by adding a picture of the client and an email if they permit.

8. Keep the process honest. Never post your own "reviews." People come to know.

9. Do not get customers to post testimonials from your office PC. All comments will show up from the same PC, and this will be quickly red-flagged by the review websites.

10. Use Google Alerts to monitor any reviews and comments about your business.

Tools and Resources

1. Spectoos - https://www.spectoos.com/ - A tool to easily collect and display customers' testimonials.

2. Clarabridge - https://www.clarabridge.com/ - Get value from every customer touchpoint. Know what your customers say and take prompt action.

3. Qualtrics - https://www.qualtrics.com/ - Qualtrics – from IBM - gives you a large number of channels for customer interaction. The platform helps you use customer feedback for product improvement and take advantage of customer feedback for every business decision.

4. Feedbackify - https://www.feedbackify.com/ - Gather ideas from customers and use their inputs to improve your products. Get to know immediately if there is a problem with your product or service.

5. Boast - https://boast.io/ - A great tool to collect, manage, and display customers' testimonials.

How to Take Advantage of Online Reviews

Why is it Important?

More than 90 percent of your customers will research your business and products/services online before they make a major purchase decision. They will search for what other people have to say about you and your ways of doing business. If they find that your business has a great reputation for professionalism, expertise, and reliability, chances are you are already halfway home to making a sale. This is the power of online reviews.

Popular review sites, such as Yelp and Google reviews, have a major effect on your sales. A single star improvement in ratings can add 10 percent to sales. Search engines may also show your review pages higher than your actual website. This will lead visitors to the review site even before they visit your web page.

Since review sites aggregate information about your business, buyers have begun to put a great amount of trust in them. For many buyers, good reviews count as much as personal recommendations. You must, therefore, work hard to ensure you have great online reviews. An extra half star can make the difference between business coming to you or going to a competitor.

Quotes from Successful People

- *"Your brand isn't what you say it is, it's what Google says it is"* — **Chris Anderson**

- *"You get a good review, and it's like crack. You need another hit. And another. And another. I know authors are like Tinkerbell and generally need applause to survive, but it's a slippery slope."* — **Alexandra Bracke**

- *"One of the best feelings in the world is reading a review by a complete stranger saying that your book is one of the best they've ever read."* — **Johnny Moscato**

- *"I love reviews. Anybody who tells you they don't read reviews is a liar."* — **Elaine Stritch**

- *"Your brand is what people say about you when you're not in the room."* — **Jeff Bezos**

10 Great Tips

1. Reading reviews is probably one of the first steps that many people take before making buying decisions. Based on some researches, 90 percent of Internet users consult online reviews before making a purchase.

2. Although there are still some issues with the review websites, many researches show that businesses that have online reviews can create more trust with their potential customers.

3. It has been proven that people trust businesses that have both negative and positive reviews more than those with only positive reviews.

4. Negative reviews can help you learn about your business issues.

5. If you see an unjust review about your business, you can explain it properly so that others can read both the review and your comment and judge.

6. One of the best techniques to get more positive reviews than negative ones is to be proactive and ask your customers' opinions and solve any potential issue in advance. You should keep in mind, however, that even if you do your best, you may still get negative reviews, so like it or not, having negative reviews is part of the game.

7. Don't only read your own business reviews. Read your competitors' reviews as well and see how you can provide a better product or service.

8. Respond to both positive and negative reviews genuinely. Don't just copy and paste the same message for everybody.

9. Don't force your customers to write reviews for you. You can indirectly mention that sharing their experience through online reviews is important for your business.

10. Avoid writing fake reviews. Review websites may remove all of your reviews, even the real ones.

Tools and Resources

1. TrustPilot - https://www.trustpilot.com/ - Build trust with customers by offering reviews that can be relied upon, contact customers using your email lists to ask for feedback on your products, and upload reviews to Google and Bing.

2. Feefo - https://www.feefo.com - Send emails to customers, analyze customer responses and reviews, display star ratings and other statistical parameters, and share your reviews on Facebook, all from a single dashboard.

3. KiyOh - https://www.kiyoh.com/ - Reasonably priced and easy to use, KiyOh also comes with alarm features to alert you in real-time about any negative reviews.

4. BazaarVoice - https://www.bazaarvoice.com/ - Hold conversations with customers instead of simply getting

reviews. BazaarVoice also accepts videos and photos to make the reviews richer and more user-friendly.

5. Survicate - https://survicate.com/ - A great tool to collect and measure your customers' satisfaction.

How to Determine if Your Marketing Activities are Effective or Not

Why is it Important?

Businesses employ several different channels for their marketing efforts. They work hard at email marketing, blogs, social media, search engine optimization, YouTube, customer testimonials, and reviews. Besides these, there are physical marketing channels as well. Your people, for example, could be visiting clients or giving demos.

It is important to understand the effectiveness and reach of each channel you are using to approach your clients. Unless you do this continuously, you will not be in a position to fine-tune your campaigns, and you could end up wasting a lot of time and money.

It is not enough to post regularly on Facebook and Instagram and think your work is done. You need to look at the effectiveness of the posts and check the leads they generate for you. It is also important to analyze the quality of the leads to see if your efforts are giving you any worthwhile input. Frequent assessment of the results of your marketing plans will let you make timely alterations.

Quotes from Successful People

- *"Focus on the core problem your business solves and put out lots of content and enthusiasm, and ideas about how to solve that problem."* — **Laura Fitton**

- *"You can't expect to just write and have visitors come to you. That's too passive."* — **Anita Campbell**

- *"Word-of-mouth marketing has always been important. Today, it's more important than ever because of the power of the Internet."* — **Joe Pulizzi & Newt Barrett**

- *"As you've noticed, people don't want to be sold. What people do want is news and information about the things they care about."* — **Larry Weber**

- *"Marketing is too important to be left to the marketing department."* — **David Packard**

10 Great Tips

1. Are your marketing activities measurable?

2. Is your staff living up to the promises they make to your customers?

3. Do you have a great level of communication with your customers?

4. Are your competitors constantly pulling ahead?

5. Do you have very low repeat customer counts?

6. Are you running in circles trying to satisfy everyone and (obviously) not succeeding?

7. Are you only relying on cutting prices to make a sale?

8. Do you use online marketing effectively?

9. Have you defined a marketing budget? How do you know it's well spent?

10. Are you abreast with what is new in the marketing world?

Tools and Resources

1. TrackMaven - https://trackmaven.com/ - Using big data analytics, TrackMaven helps you calculate the return on your marketing investment. Know instantly how successful your marketing efforts are.

2. Google Analytics - https://www.google.com/analytics/ - This free tool from Google analyzes your website activity and lets you see exactly how successful your market efforts are. You get detailed statistics and insights and native connectivity to Google Adwords.

3. Crazy Egg - https://www.crazyegg.com/ - This easy-to-use tool lets you see what visitors do when they get to your website. You know exactly which pages they visit, what links they click on, and which content they spend time on.

4. Doppler - https://www.fromdoppler.com/ - An email marketing tool that comes with several features that help you monitor the effectiveness of your marketing campaigns. Integrates natively with Google Analytics to give you rich, insightful results.

5. Tweetdeck - https://tweetdeck.twitter.com/ - This is a free tool provided by Twitter to manage your Twitter-based marketing campaign. Manage many accounts, create filters and searches, and follow brand mentions and keywords.

How to Use Videos to Market Your Business

Why is it Important?

Many businesses now understand that using video to market themselves is an important path to success. Businesses that use video in marketing discover that the cost of production of good quality material is low, the audience reach is large, and conversation rates are high. You do not have to make the video studio quality. Just an honest demonstration of your product and its use can often be good enough.

Adding a video to your marketing effort can increase the probability of success several times over. Some experts say that the probability of getting the first page on Google search can increase by a significant margin if you include video on your home page (Google owns YouTube). People are impatient and want to keep moving on, but a well-designed video can help you retain visitors a little longer on your website, and that can make a major difference in your sales.

Quotes from Successful People

- *"Business decision makers LOVE online video because it gives them the most amount of information in the shortest amount of time."* — **Robert Weiss**

- *"There is something about video marketing that helps it stay apart from the other online marketing tactics. When done correctly, all you need is one video marketing campaign to build up highly targeted traffic for a really long time."* — **Carey Lowe**

- *"Humans are incredibly visual and powerful, moving images help us find meaning . . . [and] video helps capture and contextualize the world around us."* — **Dan Patterson**

- *"Many of us have become more comfortable learning visually. Delivering information on a product, service or company through video can help to keep your audience's attention longer and make what you have to say more easily understood."* — **Savannah Stewart**

- *"Videos can attract a different audience, one that might not want to take the time to read a white paper or an article."* — **Brick Marketing**

10 Great Tips

1. If you own a small business and it is not yet well known, using video can give your business personality and credibility.

2. Use video for customer testimonials and show how customers use your product.

3. Demonstrate to people how to use your product or service. You can also showcase your infrastructure and your highly skilled staff.

4. Ensure that your video is shot in 1080p HD resolution, which is standard today. Use a collar microphone to ensure

that the audio is clear, and invest in or rent good-quality video equipment.

5. The setting must be well chosen, the script rehearsed, and several videos should be recorded before selecting and combining them into a well-polished video. If there is any doubt about your internal capability, use professionals to record the video.

6. Tag your videos so that they are found with ease in online searches. For example, if you enjoy kitchen gardens, then a search for commonly used terms associated with kitchen gardens must produce hits on your video.

7. Check that the video is not too large and can open quickly. If you can manage it, produce the same video in high definition and standard format. If customers have a fast Internet connection, they can see the video in high-definition mode. Remember that if the video takes too long to run, the customer will simply click away.

8. Keep it simple and short. Most basic videos should get the fundamental message across in less than a minute and not exceed two minutes in length.

9. Include a call to action. All your videos must end with a call to action. Suggest to clients what you want them to do. You have taken the pains and gone through considerable expenditure to produce a great video about your product. So what? Your video must (1) make clear how it will help prospective clients achieve their business goals, and (2) have a call to action that makes the client engage with you.

10. You can link to your video from several locations. Use such online sites as YouTube, Hulu, and iTunes. Put links on your blogs and social media sites where you have a presence.

Tools and Resources

1. Vyond - https://www.vyond.com/ - Earlier known as GoAnimate, Vyond is an easy-to-use, powerful tool to create marketing videos. Create animated GIF or MP4 files fast. Use

video/animation to connect with your audience and explain complex concepts.

2. Slidely - http://slide.ly/ - Create videos with ease that is astounding. Promote your business using video that you can customize with your logo and text.

3. Wideo - https://wideo.co/ - Create video even if you have zero experience in video creation. Wideo comes with a large number of ready-to-use templates that make your work easy.

4. ViewBix - http://corp.viewbix.com/ - Create interactive video ads on the ViewBix platform. You can integrate this tool with your email marketing efforts and share the video on any platform/device.

5. Vimeo - www.vimeo.com/business - With Vimeo for Business, you get the capability to load up to 7 TB of video without any weekly limits. Organize your video library all in one place and get professional video marketing capabilities.

How to Use HootSuite to Save a lot of Time in Social Media Marketing

Why is it Important?

HootSuite is what is called a comprehensive social media management system. These days businesses have a large social media presence. This can mean managing dozens of different platforms, such as Facebook, Twitter, Instagram, LinkedIn, and many others. If you want to use all of these channels successfully, you will have to stay vigilant and manage each of these in near real-time. This can mean a lot of time wasted checking for messages and comments. HootSuite allows you to manage all your social media accounts in a single place, thereby saving you a lot of time and effort.

You can also use HootSuite to manage many different media channels on the same platform. For example, you could be having several different Facebook pages dealing with different products or activities. HootSuite allows you to manage all of these pages from a single screen. This ensures that you can respond rapidly to customers and give the impression of an agile and efficient business.

HootSuite also has features that allow you to distribute tasks between different members of your social media management team. Once your social media marketing plan grows beyond a certain size, this is an inescapable feature.

Quotes from Successful People

- *"As technology advances, it reverses the characteristics of every situation again and again. The age of automation is going to be the age of do it yourself."* — **Marshall McLuhan**

- *"Automation is good, so long as you know exactly where to put the machine."* — **Eliyahu Goldratt**

- *"I use social media as an idea generator, trend mapper and strategic compass for all of our online business ventures."* — **Paul Barron**

- *"We have technology, finally, that for the first time in human history allows people to really maintain rich connections with much larger numbers of people."* — **Pierre Omidyar**

- *"Content Doesn't Win. Optimized Content Wins."* — **Liana Evans**

10 Great Tips

1. HootSuite allows you to connect most of the well-known social networks, such as Facebook, LinkedIn, Twitter, and Instagram to a single platform, so you can post in all connected networks through one HootSuite account.

2. HootSuite also allows you to schedule all your posts ahead of time. As an example, you can schedule all your weekly posts every Sunday.

3. You can create teams with different members to manage your social media marketing from one platform.

4. You can get great analytical reports to determine the effectiveness of your social media campaigns.

5. You can create different streams and tabs to learn more about industry trends, top influencers, and your competitors.

6. You can search on social networks more effectively.

7. You can assign social network posts to your team.

8. You can review and approve your team members' posts before publishing.

9. You can shorten lengthy web links by sharing them through HootSuite.

10. You can use the HootSuite App to conduct all your social media marketing through your cell phone.

Tools and Resources

1. Reddit Keyword Monitor Pro - https://apps.hootsuite.com/ - (Type Reddit Keyword in the search area) - A free tool for HootSuite enterprise users, Reddit Keyword Monitor Pro gives you customizable features that let you work across your social networks and gives you quality analytics.

2. Syndicator Pro - https://apps.hootsuite.com/ - (Type Syndicator Pro in the search area) - This tool gives you an easy way to monitor RSS feeds and Google alerts and share them with your social media accounts.

3. Reputology - https://apps.hootsuite.com/ - (Type Reputology in the search area) - A free app from HootSuite that lets you monitor your ratings on a wide variety of social media platforms and see them all together. Saves you time and money and lets you respond faster than ever before.

4. Insights - https://apps.hootsuite.com/- (Type Insights in the search area) - Make smarter business decisions with Insights.

Use a large number of data sources and get real-time results that you can use immediately.

5. Brandwatch - https://apps.hootsuite.com/ - (Type Brandwatch in the search area) - Get inputs from millions of traffic sources on the Internet on a single interface and use the data to make better business decisions.

How to Have a Strategic Marketing Plan

Why is it Important?

A Strategic Marketing Plan is important to ensure that you run your business according to a plan and do not get sidetracked into making ad hoc decisions. The plan allows you to see the big picture and ensures that even if you are forced to make changes due to circumstances, you can quickly get your business back on track.

Once you have decided on a strategic marketing plan, you will be able to detect distractions and avoid getting sidetracked easily. This will ensure that your resources are not wasted on fads of the moment but are used in the most efficient way possible.

Creating a strategic marketing plan forces you to analyze your budget, areas of focus, customer groups, and target markets. It helps you create a solid foundation for future growth. Smart businesses understand which elements of their marketing plan should be flexible and which should be rigid. This allows them to take advantage of changing circumstances and yet stay on the path to meeting long-term goals. Spending time to create a strategic marketing plan is one activity you cannot afford to miss.

Quotes from Successful People

- *"The aim of marketing is to know and understand the customer so well the product or service fits him and sells itself."* — **Peter Drucker**

- *"In marketing I've seen only one strategy that can't miss—to market to your best customers first."* — **John Romero**

- *"If you form a strategy without research, your brand will barely float and at the speed industries move at today brands sink fast."* — **Ryan Holmes**

- *"The customer expects you to have knowledge of their stuff, not just your stuff."* — **Jeffrey Gitomer**

- *"The first step in exceeding your customer's expectations is to know those expectations."* — **Roy H. Williams**

10 Great Tips

1. Strategic marketing planning is the road map to improving your profitability and developing satisfying relationships with your customers. Both new and established businesses need to work on a comprehensive marketing plan to ensure that their business grows in their target markets.

2. Seen in the light of today's economy, spending time and effort on a well-structured marketing plan can make all the difference between a successful marketing run and a failed one.

3. You should arrive at a carefully designed framework that acts as a reference for your budgeting, customer service, and course of action.

4. The first and most important step in any strategic marketing plan is setting business goals. Clearly defined business goals are critical to keeping your efforts focused.

5. Follow the SMART (Specific, Measurable, Attainable, Relevant, and Time-bound) principle while formulating goals.

6. Break your long-term goals into small-term goals. When these are achieved, your long-term goals are automatically met.

7. Although strategic marketing planning essentially deals with marketing, it actually involves analyzing all the external components that affect your business. The main idea behind

effective marketing decisions is to provide better or more services/products than your competition offers.

8. The process involves collecting marketing information in a systematic manner and then integrating that data into a detailed analysis that helps project long-term marketing goals.

9. Your strategic marketing plan must cover as long a time horizon as you can be comfortable with; however, it is also a fact that many things will change with time, so there has to be an element of flexibility in the plan as well.

10. A strategic marketing plan offers a two-pronged advantage to business owners: (1) it helps you drive valuable funds and resources toward desired marketing goals (while preventing them from flowing into unproductive markets), and (2) it minimizes wasting money and time.

Tools and Resources

1. Airtable - https://airtable.com/ - A great tool to develop marketing plans and many other projects.

2. Marketing Donut - https://www.marketingdonut.co.uk/ - Use Marketing Donut to understand your market and create a winning marketing action plan.

3. Brainrider - https://www.brainrider.com/ - Use Brainrider's Accounts Based Strategy to get better ROI and achieve all your business targets. Get your sales and marketing teams on the same page and focus on the accounts that really matter.

4. Smartsheet - https://www.smartsheet.com - Use the free marketing strategy templates to set goals and identify resources required to achieve them. The template ensures you do not miss out on any important aspect of strategic planning.

5. Alexa - https://www.alexa.com/ - A great tool to find, reach, and convert your audience.

How to Have a Great Website

Why is it Important?

Very often, your website will be the first point of contact your business will have with a prospective customer. If you have created an unprofessional, low-quality website, then no prizes for guessing what the customer will think about your business. Customers will not waste their time on a badly designed website. They will take one look and move on.

Good websites load fast, have great content, and tell a story that binds the attention of visitors. They are very efficient in their purpose and let customers get whatever they need with the least fuss. If the workflow is smooth and simple, you will find greater customer retention as compared with a site where users have to scratch their heads to figure out what to do.

Even brick-and-mortar businesses require a quality website. This is because most customers search for information online. If you do not have an online presence, you could be losing business even when your buyers are sitting next door to you.

Quotes from Successful People

- *"What separates design from art is that design is meant to be . . . functional."* — **Cameron Moll**

- *"To become successful online, you only need to remember the following : Good Heart + Passion + Web Design + SEO + Digital Marketing + Dedication + Positiveness + Patience = Success"* — **Dr. Christopher Dayagdag**

- *"Responsive Web Design always plays important role whenever going to promote your website."* — **Josh Wilson**

- *"Website without visitors is like a ship lost in the horizon."* — **Dr. Christopher Dayagdag**

- *"Web design is not just about creating pretty layouts. It's about understanding the marketing challenge behind your business."* — **Mohamed Saad**

10 Great Tips

1. Just as you would care about designing your shop or office space to make it attractive and functional, your website (and consequently your business) also benefits from state-of-the-art web design.

2. When you start building your website, you should be clear about its target audience and the kind of content they would be looking for. The website must add to your business by becoming a channel of communication with prospective customers.

3. Why do you need to set up this website? What are you hoping to accomplish with it, and how will it contribute to your business?

4. Optimum web design essentially combines excellent functionality and aesthetic design. Translated into simple language, your business website must be able to attract customers to click on your website and then be able to offer them options of buying your product online or contacting you for information.

5. The website must be easy to use (all your customers are not going to be computer nerds) and must WORK. Every link to any data that you want to make available must work 100 percent of the time.

6. Choose an eye-catching title or header that attracts the reader's attention at once. Split your information into smaller bits so that it is easy to navigate and understand.

7. Not everyone is a fan of blinking adverts. They can become an annoyance if overdone. If you do like having them, see that they turn themselves off after a short while. Keep banners, ads, and links optional. Offer a clear and

comprehensive site chart that allows readers to navigate your website according to their pace and wish.

8. Display your business phone numbers, address, and email address on your website. Websites that lack contact details appear dubious. You might want to ensure that you come across as a real person with a real product or service to offer your customers.

9. Collect a list of questions that you are asked most frequently from those who look at your products or services. If you cannot compile such a list, ask your customers through an informal survey.

10. List the problems that your product/service should solve. List the benefits that your customers get from using your product/service.

Tools and Resources

1. Wix - https://www.wix.com/ - Gives you many different methods to design a great website. Good for pros as well as those new to the job.

2. Webnode - https://us.webnode.com/ - 30 million users use Webnode to build great websites complete with shopping carts and payment methods.

3. IM Creator - http://www.imcreator.com/ - Build websites like a pro. IM Creator gives you white-labeled websites that you can customize and use in minutes.

4. Site 123 - http://www.site123.com/ - If you want to get your site up fast, try Site 123. It comes with ready-made layouts and styles that will fit most needs.

5. Weebly - https://www.weebly.com - With drag and drop functionality and no-coding approach, Weebly will get you going whether you want a store or a blog.

How to Create an Effective Blog?

Why is it Important?

A blog is one of the simplest yet effective marketing devices you could have. Blogs started as an expression of thoughts on a website that anyone could access. Today, however, business-related blogs have become a prime tool in driving traffic to your website, improving your website's ranking on search engines, and getting you recognized as an expert in your field.

A blog allows you to interact with people who have an interest in your product or service. As your blog becomes popular, people will begin commenting on and discussing what they have shared. This creates a buzz about your product and directs very high-quality traffic to your website. Over time, the traffic to your blog will move on to your website and add to sales.

A good blog on a specific subject establishes you as an expert in the field. It lets readers see that you are updated with the latest information about your products or services. Over time, your blog gets a good reputation, and people begin referring to it regularly. People share such blog posts, and your business gains immensely from such publicity.

Quotes from Successful People

- *"Don't focus on having a great blog. Focus on producing a blog that's great for your readers."* — **Brian Clark**

- *"The first thing you need to decide when you build your blog is what you want to accomplish with it, and what it can do if successful."* — **Ron Dawson**

- *"There are tons of different factors that go into ranking well, but the biggest is high-quality content."* — **David Sinick**

- *"If you want to continually grow your blog, you need to learn to blog on a consistent basis."* — **Neil Patel**

- *"There's a lot of information out there for free, so you've got to figure out what makes your information different."* — **Matt Wolfe**

10 Great Tips

1. Blogging has been around for a long time and is an extremely effective tool to create a footprint for you and demonstrate an area of expertise. If you maintain a great blog, your customers will be convinced that you have a very deep knowledge of your field and that you keep abreast of the latest developments in the area.

2. Since you are writing to attract prospective customers, the blog has to discuss your subject in detail and demonstrate to prospective customers that you know the subject well and that they can rely on your judgment.

3. Plan your blog. If you have many different things on your mind, don't jumble them in a single blog. Write separate posts instead. Think about what you are going to write. Start a day before you plan to post.

4. Work to an outline when you write; it makes your job easier. Use simple English, short sentences, and small paragraphs.

5. Do not blog randomly. Discuss a small number of subjects in a blog so that your blog does not lose focus, and the reader knows what to expect.

6. Keep your content fresh. If possible, try to post content that will not be outdated very soon.

7. Make it easy for your readers to comment and discuss issues arising from what you write.

8. Make it easy for readers to share your content with their friends. Using Facebook, Twitter, and emailing blog entries is very easy.

9. Post weekly if not more often.

10. Use social network buttons on your blog; put the buttons after every entry so people can share your content on their social networks.

Tools and Resources

1. Wordpress - https://wordpress.com/ - With a little bit of effort, you can build a great blog on the Wordpress platform. A very large number of plugins are available for easy customization and functionality.

2. Square Space - http://www.squarespace.com/ - If you want to create a blog in next to no time, Lookup Square Space. Easy to set up and use, even for complete novices.

3. BuzzSumo - http://buzzsumo.com/ - Get your creative juices flowing with BuzzSumo—see what is trending in your domain and how others are writing about it.

4. Keyword Tool - http://keywordtool.io/ - Enter a search term and Keyword Tool will give you a vast number of alternative ideas related to your term. Use the power of Google's autocompleting feature to get keyword suggestions.

5. PhotoPin - http://photopin.com/ - Want a copyright-free image for your blog? Go to PhotoPin and get your blog going. You can also search for sponsored images if you are willing to pay for them.

How to Use the Basic Search Engine Optimization Techniques

Why is it Important?

Many small-business owners may not realize this, but Search Engine Optimization (SEO) can mean the difference between failure and success. When you are working in a small geographical area and competing with large organizations, effective SEO can ensure that local customers get to know about you and get their business to you rather than to the large chains.

Like it or not, customers have faith in search engine results. If Google places you on the first page of a search output, you can be sure that you will get a disproportionate amount of traffic as compared with a competitor who is on page five. In such a case, the possibility of converting visits into sales is very high.

When SEO drives traffic to your website, you get access to great insights from Google Analytics and similar tools. You get to know the profile of the persons who visit your pages and what their interests are. This allows you to target your customer base better and achieve better sales. It has been proven that good SEO makes great business sense. Start paying more attention to SEO today!

Quotes from Successful People

- *"Good SEO work only gets better over time. It's only search engine tricks that need to keep changing when the ranking algorithms change."* — **Jill Whalen**

- *"Google only loves you when everyone else loves you first."* — **Wendy Piersall**

- *"Today it's not about 'get the traffic'—it's about 'get the targeted and relevant traffic.'"* — **Adam Audette**

- *"Better content is outweighing more content."* — **Rand Fishkin**

- *"What gets measured gets improved."* — **Peter Drucker**

10 Great Tips

1. SEO or Search Engine Optimization refers to creating and setting up your website content so that search engines, such as Google, Yahoo!, and Bing, can show your site on the first page of their search results.

2. SEO is the partnering link between your website and the search engine. The stronger the SEO, the better the chances of being picked up by the search engine and, consequently the customer.

3. Use targeted keywords and keyword phrases: If, for example, your business involves selling stationery, your keywords could be pen(s), stapler(s), paper, office stationery, stationery, and several others.

4. Keep your content useful and relevant to your customer. Keywords must be embedded in a skillful and meaningful manner. Rambling and "filler" texts will send the reader away in less than ten seconds.

5. SEO not only involves using relevant and targeted keywords but also placing them correctly to enhance the value of your website content. Keep the content on your web pages fresh and change it regularly. Allow your visitors to discuss and comment since this adds to your keyword density and helps you rise in search engine rankings.

6. Know your target audience completely. Many business owners focus so hard on their business or product that they forget their customers. Your website has to anticipate the actions of the prospective customer.

7. You have to understand core keywords and their use to ensure that your website scores high with search engines. Crude methods, such as stuffing your web pages with keywords, are counterproductive. Search engines are smart and penalize you for such tactics.

8. Have your website built professionally and make it easy to search and index. While graphics and visual themes are important, ensure that text descriptors are present that search engines can understand.

9. Setting up a blog on your website is a great way to ensure that your keywords are repeated and used a large number of times naturally without making it appear contrived.

10. Connect your website to your social networks. Update your Instagram, Facebook, LinkedIn, and Twitter pages. Try to get readers involved and active on your social media pages.

Tools and Resources

1. Google Search Console - https://search.google.com/search-console/about - Use the power of Google itself to create Google-friendly websites. This can save you hours of wasted work.

2. Screaming Frog - https://www.screamingfrog.co.uk/seo-spider/ - An indispensable tool for website designers. Screaming Frog will analyze your site and its metadata to determine if there is any optimization you can do to improve your site.

3. SEMRush - https://www.semrush.com/ - Improve the quality of your SEO, get access to quality analytics, and analyze backlinks and your keyword use. Best for those with some experience of SEO.

4. Moz - https://moz.com/free-seo-tools - A great tool to do search engine optimization.

5. HubSpot SEO - https://www.hubspot.com/ - Not only does it help you in optimizing your site, but it is also a great learning resource as well.

How to Use Email Marketing

Why is it Important?

Many small-business owners feel that with the emergence of other marketing tools, email marketing days are over. They are wrong. With more than half of the entire world's population using email, email marketing has the best return on investment by a wide margin.

Advertisements on TV and print media have become expensive and lack results. Advertising on search engines and social media can be very expensive. On the other hand, if you have taken the pains to build an email list of people who use or are interested in using your product, then reaching these people is very easy and cost-effective by email. Using your email list, you can segment your audience very precisely and handle each segment specifically. This ensures that the response rate to an email campaign can be very high.

Very often, customers are on the move and may only have their smartphone with them, but your emails can still reach them. Since most people use their smartphones to check email several times a day, you can be sure that your message will be seen even when people are away from their desks.

Unlike many other marketing techniques, email marketing can be highly automated. This allows you to run a campaign with minimal resources. You can create workflows where automatic responses are given to customer inputs and follow up with more personalized responses. This ensures greater customer connect and improved sales.

Quotes from Successful People

- *"Email has an ability many channels don't: creating valuable, personal touches—at scale."* — **David Newman**

- *"Signing up is a powerful signal of intent to buy. Send them email until they do."* — **Jordie van Rijn**

- *"Quality over quantity—Emails may best cost efficient but it's no excuse to not produce quality content to give to a targeted audience."* — **Benjamin Murray**

- *"A small list that wants exactly what you're offering is better than a bigger list that isn't committed."* — **Ramsay Leimenstoll**

- *"Start testing and stop arguing."* — **Jon Correll**

10 Great Tips

1. Write your mail well. The reader will glance at your message, so make sure every word counts.

2. Ensure that the key points of your message can be understood in the first hundred words because, in all probability, the reader will see the message in a small preview window.

3. Provide at least one link to your website in the first hundred words.

4. Do not rely on images to send your message since most browsers do not display images in emails by default.

5. Do not harass the reader. Make it easy for them to unsubscribe from your mailing list.

6. Create test accounts on the major email sites and check out your message on all of these before sending it to real clients.

7. In all of your emails, remember that the message must be customized to the intended reader. Successful email marketing does not start with blasting off a thousand emails to an address list. You will be lucky if you get one reply. On the other hand, well-crafted emails personalized to the recipient will get you a far better response rate.

8. Make your mail interesting. Give a good offer right at the start to hold the reader's interest.

9. Monitor your statistics. What is your email open rate? If this changes drastically, you should investigate immediately because you could have been labeled a spammer, and your mails may have been stopped.

10. Keep your mails frequent but not irritatingly so. About once a week is OK. If the mail pertains to work, send it on Wednesdays or Thursdays. If it is about leisure, try Saturdays or Sundays.

Tools and Resources

1. Constant Contact - https://www.constantcontact.com - An easy-to-use email marketing service that is ideal for those who are just starting off. This platform comes with templates, list management systems, image libraries, and more features.

2. Drip - https://www.drip.com/ - A powerful email platform that is ideal for e-commerce companies. The smart email marketing platform is equipped with a large variety of tools that help you reach specified audiences.

3. ConvertKit - https://convertkit.com/ - One of the easiest to use email marketing tools it allows you to set autoresponders as well as set up drip emails. ConvertKit allows easy segmentation and management of your email lists.

4. Aweber - https://www.aweber.com/ - Ideally suited for small and medium-sized businesses, Aweber comes with a long list of tools that help you get productive fast. Get detailed insights with great analytics.

5. GetResponse - https://www.getresponse.com/ - A very popular solution for all your email marketing needs. Ideal for those starting off new and for small/medium businesses. GetResponse integrates easily with many lead-generating solutions.

How to Have Excellent Customer Service

Why is it Important?

Businesses that offer high-quality customer service are able to build favorable customer opinions and get valuable feedback that allows the business to improve further. Proactive businesses use good customer relations to catch problems before they become serious and correct them before issues become widespread. It is well known that selling to an existing customer is far easier than getting a new one. High-quality customer service ensures that your customers stay loyal to you.

Businesses that have a good connection with their customers will take steps to ensure that the customer is ordering the correct variant of their product and using it the right way. Good businesses will even tell customers when a product is not suited to their needs. This ensures much better customer satisfaction and improves your reputation in the market.

Even though there will be occasional problems with products and services, businesses that treat their customers with respect and take rapid action to resolve issues will get customer loyalty. Customers understand that problems can occur. They want to see problems resolved fast and be treated courteously.

Businesses with a strong culture of great customer service often have very good relations between various branches of the business itself. Everyone understands the value of promptness, courtesy, and decent behavior. As a result, there is harmony within the business as well. This is guaranteed to lead to business success.

Quotes from Successful People

- *"People don't care how much you know until they know how much you care."* — **Theodore Roosevelt**

- *"Even your most loyal customers always have a choice about where to take their business."* — **Marilyn Suttle**

- *"In the old world, you devoted 30% of your time to building a great service and 70% of your time to shouting about it. In the new world, that inverts."* — **Jeff Bezos**

- *"Understanding who isn't your ideal customer sometimes helps you better clarify who is."* — **Amber Hurdle**

- *"A satisfied customer is the best business strategy of all."* — **Michael LeBoeuf**

10 Great Tips

1. You can make the best product possible and sell it for as low a price as you can, but if you cannot get your customers to stay with you and also maintain a positive image of your service, you won't last long in the market.

2. It has been calculated that it takes eight times the effort and expense to acquire a new customer as it does to keep an old one. That is how important good customer service can be!

3. One key element of customer service is the gap between promise and delivery. If this gap exists—you are in trouble.

4. Any forward-thinking company will go the extra mile for its customers, knowing very well that every customer—no matter how small—is critical.

5. Have someone answer the phone within three rings every time. You could use call forwarding or hire an answering service, but you should ensure that a person is present (not a recorded voice) available when your customer or potential customer rings. Similar rules apply to emails. Every email has to be responded to within a few hours and not more than twenty-four.

6. Make only those promises that you are sure you will be able to keep. This requirement turns up in many places (including personal relationships), and it is critical in business too. If you make a promise, you keep it no matter what may happen.

7. Handle complaints promptly. Every time you hear a complaint, remember how much more it will cost you to get a new customer and then work hard on retaining the one with the problem.

8. Be genuinely helpful. By going the extra mile for your customers, you will develop a lifelong relationship. In fact, do not even wait until the person becomes a customer. Every person you meet or contact is a potential customer. Many companies coach their employees to not simply say "in room 211" when someone asks them for directions. Instead, you should walk with the person to room 211.

9. Ensure your staff shows the same courtesy as you do to your customers. There are times when workers may not be on the same page as you are about customer care. Take time to coach them and take feedback from your customers. Remember this—everyone from the lift operator to the CEO is working for the same company.

10. When the customer speaks, keep quiet and listen. Many people tend to get defensive and argue their point. This is a fundamental error. Let customers have their say and listen very carefully. Treat every complaint as feedback; take it seriously and find the underlying cause

Tools and Resources

1. Zendesk - https://www.zendesk.com/ - Zendesk is a complete solution for all your customer care requirements. Beautifully and intuitively designed, Zendesk components can be bought all together or individually.

2. Freshdesk - https://freshdesk.com/ - Set up a call center in no time at all, get full ticketing support, create a knowledge base, and much more. Fresh\desk is fun to use, even for your staff.

3. Helpdesk - https://www.ladesk.com/ - Specifically built for small and medium businesses, this platform is full-featured, low cost, and supports call center-like activities. You can even set quotas for your customer service agents.

4. Groove - https://www.groovehq.com/ - A simple help desk solution that integrates easily with any popular email service. It comes ready to use with detailed analytics that helps you understand your business better.

5. Help Scout - https://www.helpscout.net/ - Easy to learn, Help Scout comes with a large number of features that help you get the best out of your help desk. A content management system is also built-in that you can use to handle queries better.

How to Impress Your Customers

Why is it Important?

Customers usually have many options for shopping. Unless you provide them with exceptional service and superior goods, they will not return to you. This is why it is critical to impress your customers—not with fancy designs and words—but with quality service and attention to detail.

All businessmen know that it is far more difficult to acquire a new customer as compared to retaining one. About 80 percent of your income comes from 20 percent of your customers. Therefore, it is critical to focus on customers and do what it takes to retain them. Businesses that understand this basic principle go all out to keep customers happy.

By impressing your customers with quality service, you ensure that you will get great word-of-mouth publicity. You will build great brand loyalty if you respond promptly to customers and handle their problems immediately. Impress your customers with quality service, and your business will grow rapidly.

Quotes from Successful People

- *"Being on par in terms of price and quality only gets you into the game. Service wins the game."* — **Tony Allesandra**

- *"Know what your customers want most and what your company does best. Focus on where those two meet."* — **Kevin Stirtz**

- *"Make your product easier to buy than your competition, or you will find your customers buying from them, not you."* — **Mark Cuban**

- *"Here is a simple but powerful rule: always give people more than what they expect to get."* — **Nelson Boswell**

- *"There are no traffic jams along the extra mile."* — **Roger Staubach**

10 Great Tips

1. Promise less, deliver more.

2. Try to understand your customers' needs rather than just fulfilling their wants.

3. Ask for their feedback.

4. Send them gifts, birthday cards, free samples, and . . .

5. Give them purchase consultations instead of trying to sell them something.

6. Never talk badly behind your competitors.

7. Learn about all similar products and services in the market.

8. Ask them to try your products before purchasing them.

9. Provide great customer service.

10. Ask their opinions about your future products or services.

Tools and Resources

1. Book: *Be Our Guest: Perfecting the Art of Customer Service,* by The Disney Institute and Theodore Kinni
   https://amzn.to/32a5Nrn

2. Book: *The Service Culture Handbook: A Step-by-Step Guide to Getting Your Employees Obsessed with Customer Service,* by Jeff Toister https://amzn.to/324yYvI

3. Book: *Customer Service Tip of the Week: Over 52 ideas and reminders to sharpen your skills,* by Jeff Toister
   https://amzn.to/3247Rkr

4. Book: *7L: The Seven Levels of Communication: Go From Relationships to Referrals,* by Michael J. Maher
   https://amzn.to/32aH5Hr

5. Book: *The Customer Rules: The 39 Essential Rules for Delivering Sensational Service*, by Lee Cockerell https://amzn.to/321R2Xq

How to Use Referral Marketing to Get Customers

Why is it Important?

Small businesses can benefit immensely from referrals from existing customers. People trust their friends and family much more than they trust advertisements. Therefore, by getting your existing customers to provide you with referrals, you have a better chance of acquiring new customers than any other way.

Most people today have social media accounts and could have large numbers of friends on social media platforms. If one such person gives your business a positive mention, many other potential users will see the message. This is a very effective way of getting more customers.

Successful businesses make it easy and rewarding for satisfied clients to provide them with referrals. This has the benefit of acting like a loyalty program where you reward your customers for giving you referrals. Using referral marketing allows you to focus on producing a great product while the clients keep coming on.

Quotes from Successful People

- *"The purpose of a business is to create a customer who creates customers."* — **Shiv Singh**

- *"Loyal customers, they don't just come back, they don't simply recommend you, they insist that their friends do business with you."* — **Chip Bell**

- *"The customer experience is the next competitive battleground."* — **Jerry Gregoire**

- *"One customer, well taken care of, could be more valuable than $10,000 worth of advertising."* — **Jim Rohn**

- *"In sales, a referral is the key to the door of resistance."* — **Bo Bennett**

10 Great Tips

1. Referral marketing is a process to encourage your current customers to talk about your products or services so that you can get new customers.

2. Due to increased competition and online information, referral marketing is one of the best ways to promote your business.

3. The main concept behind referral marketing is trust. How can you create a trustworthy relationship with your current customers so that they can refer you?

4. Referral marketing includes the following four steps:

   a. Helping people learn about your products or services

   b. Allowing people to try your products or giving them free consultations

   c. Delivering more than you promised during the purchase time and having great customer service

   d. Being in touch with customers and asking for referrals

5. Using social networks and meeting people in person are the two main channels of introducing your products or services.

6. Providing free samples and allowing people to try your products or services before the final purchase creates more trust.

7. Educate your customers about the benefits of your products or services. Inform people about the factors they need to consider if they want to buy this type of product or service.

8. Deliver more than you promised to impress your customers.

9. Do not forget your customers after selling. Always add great customer services and follow up with them.

10. Ask your current customers to refer you, new customers, whenever they are so happy with your products or services.

Tools and Resources

1. Post Affiliate Pro - https://www.postaffiliatepro.com - Start a free trial and upgrade later. Post Affiliate Pro is a full-featured solution with advanced features. An ideal solution for small businesses or start-ups. Associate unlimited numbers of affiliates and let your business grow.

2. Refersion - https://www.refersion.com - Complete control over your referral program; also allow your customers to refer their friends through social media, email, and other channels. Completely customizable.

3. Tapfiliate - https://tapfiliate.com - An affiliate marketing solution that is specifically focused on the e-commerce industry. Customize it to build the solution you want whether you are a small business or a multinational.

4. Referral Rock - https://referralrock.com/ - A proven solution that works like a charm for any business model. Expand your referral activities with this easy-to-use, popular solution.

5. Book: *The Referral Engine: Teaching Your Business to Market Itself*, by John Jantsch https://amzn.to/324z9am

How to Network Like a Pro

Why is it Important?

You may have heard, "your network is your net worth." Small-business owners need to network with each other and with their customers and collaborators. The key benefits that come from developing good networking are discussed below.

Networking helps you develop business leads. As you build networks, you will get to know about new opportunities and new ideas that will help you add additional dimensions to your business. The network helps your business grow.

Building strong networks will give you exposure to the best practices other people follow. They may not necessarily be in the same line of work as you are, but knowing what methods and techniques other businesses follow will help you make your business more efficient and progressive.

When you attend industry events and interact closely with other professionals, you get to know the latest trends in your field before they become common knowledge. This helps you to stay at the leading edge in your industry.

Quotes from Successful People

- *"Becoming well known (at least among your prospects & connections) is the most valuable element in the connection process."* — **Jeffrey Gitomer**

- *"Pulling a good network together takes effort, sincerity and time."* — **Alan Collins**

- *"You can make more friends in two months by becoming interested in other people than you can in two years by trying to get other people interested in you."* — **Dale Carnegie**

- *"The currency of real networking is not greed but generosity."* — **Keith Ferrazzi**

- *"Networking is an investment in your business. It takes time and when done correctly can yield great results for years to come."* — **Diane Helbig**

10 Great Tips

1. Networking is one of the most important elements of success in both personal and professional life. You may have heard that "your network is your net worth!"

2. Don't forget to follow up after meeting new people. Your networking is not effective if you do not follow up and maintain your connections.

3. Finding the best way to help a person is the best method to connect with him or her. Always give before ask!

4. Try to be an intriguing and visible person so that people will be encouraged to learn more about you. If people do not know about you, how can they do business with you?

5. Think of people as humans, not just business opportunities. Trust is the foundation of all types of relationships.

6. Try to meet and learn about as many people as you can in an event. Do not just stay with one person during the whole event.

7. Attend local networking events at least twice a month. Based on your profession, attend national and international events as well.

8. Connect with people through social networks but also meet them in person since online connections are not as strong as knowing people in person.

9. Use professional group websites, event platforms, such as Eventbrite.com, and social networks to find your industry-related events.

10. Diversify your network. Do not just connect with one group of people in terms of ethnicity, locations, and professions.

Tools and Resources

1. Lifograph - https://www.lifograph.com/ - Get detailed data about people who matter in Silicon Valley. Discover

connections between people and see how connections have developed over time.

2. Let's Lunch - https://letslunch.com/ - Network with people who matter to your business. Let's Lunch helps you connect and organize meetings.

3. CircleBack - https://www.circleback.com/ - Make contact management easy with CircleBack. Connects natively to your CRM tool so that you can get the most out of your contacts and build stronger professional relationships.

4. FullContact - https://www.fullcontact.com/ - Get more out of your contacts using identity resolution. Start with basic information about people and get rich details about them without leaving your desktop.

5. Book: *How to Talk to Anyone: 92 Little Tricks for Big Success in Relationships*, by Leil Lowndes https://amzn.to/2KWWtS0

How to Close a Sale

Why is it Important?

The essence of running a good business is in selling quality products or services and keeping customers satisfied. If you do not learn the art of closing deals, there is no way you can grow your business.

Closing a sale demands careful attention to strategies. Different clients think differently, and your salespeople must be adept at dealing with them individually. Every major deal will not go your way. Some clients will be difficult and demand concessions and bargain hard. A wise businessman knows what he can compromise on and what needs to be maintained rigidly.

There is a greater chance of closing a sale if you keep your deals as simple as possible. Use plain language and transparent terms so that the client can understand what you are saying without any ambiguity. Simpler deals give your clients confidence and help close sales faster.

You will find you can close sales faster if you pay close attention to what the client says. If you understand client requirements completely, chances are you will be able to offer a complete solution that closes deals and adds to your bottom line.

Quotes from Successful People

- *"You don't close a sale, you open a relationship if you want to build a long-term, successful enterprise."* — **Patricia Fripp**

- *"Every sale has five basic obstacles: no need, no money, no hurry, no desire, no trust."* — **Zig Ziglar**

- *"Most people think 'selling' is the same as 'talking.' But the most effective salespeople know that listening is the most important part of their job."* — **Roy Bartell**

- *"Ninety percent of selling is conviction and 10 percent is persuasion."* — **Shiv Khera**

- *"Plan the sale when you plan the ad."* — **Leo Burnett**

10 Great Tips

1. Keep in mind that trust is the foundation of every relationship.

2. Learn about the 5Cs (Company, Customers, Competitors, Collaborates, Climate of the market) of your business.

3. Give a purchase consultation instead of pushing your customers to buy your products or services.

4. Talk about all social, economic, and cultural (market trends), especially regarding that specific industry. Show that you are knowledgeable in this field.

5. Learn and focus on your customers' needs. Ask insightful questions to learn about them.

6. Explain to your customer how his/her needs will be satisfied by using your products or services.

7. Ask your customers to take a piece of paper and write down all the pros and cons of your products or services.

8. Offer your customers a chance to try your products or services.

9. Provide an effective warranty or return policy.

10. Provide different options for your customers. Do not go for "take it or leave it."

Tools and Resources

1. Mixpanel - https://mixpanel.com/ - Understand user requirements and determine which of your processes increase customer engagement, retention, and conversion. Make completely data-driven decisions.

2. Recurly - https://recurly.com/ - If your sales follow the subscription-based model, Recurly is the solution you need. Built specifically for small-scale business, it offers a simple payment and subscription management tool.

3. Book: *How To Be A GREAT Salesperson...By Monday Morning!: If You Want to Increase Your Sales Read This Book. It is That Simple*, by David R Cook https://amzn.to/2HtjVE5

4. Book: *The Introvert's Edge: How the Quiet and Shy Can Outsell Anyone*, by Matthew Pollard https://amzn.to/2KX1lGF

5. Book: *How I Raised Myself From Failure To Success In Selling*, by Frank Bettger https://amzn.to/2ZrBqz0

How to keep in Touch with Customers

Why is it Important?

All business people know that it is much harder (and more costly) acquiring a new customer as compared with retaining an existing one. Staying in touch with your customers on a regular basis ensures you get repeat business, referrals, and loyalty.

The database of customers that you may have built is a treasure trove. Do not use it simply to send out birthday or anniversary greetings. Smart businesses know their lean months, and they often offer customers a discounted rate on their services. This ensures that the workforce does not become idle and that the cash keeps flowing in.

Keeping in regular touch with your customers also ensures that the name of your business stays fresh in their minds. In a real estate business, for example, you may not get much repeat business, but if satisfied customers remember you, they are more likely to recommend you if a friend needs to buy a house.

Connect with customers at a deeper level and form strong bonds with them. This is one long-proven way to marketing success.

Quotes from Successful People

- *"When dealing with people, remember you are not dealing with creatures of logic, but creatures of emotion."* — **Dale Carnegie**

- *"The more you engage with customers the clearer things become and the easier it is to determine what you should be doing."* — **John Russell**

- *"As you've noticed, people don't want to be sold. What people do want is news and information about the things they care about."* — **Larry Weber**

- *"The first step in exceeding your customer's expectations is to know those expectations."* — **Roy H. Williams**

- *"Every contact we have with a customer influences whether or not they'll come back. We have to be great every time or we'll lose them."* — **Kevin Stirtz**

10 Great Tips

1. Create a database of your customers and keep their information as much as you can, such as date of birth, anniversary, and . . .

2. Send them online newsletters with useful information.

3. Give them a call once of while to see if they are still using your products or services or just to say hi.

4. Make social network connections with your customers.

5. Send them gift cards and birthday notes.

6. Provide free training to use your products effectively.

7. Meet them in person.

8. Send them your new offers.

9. Follow up with surveys regarding your products/services.

10. Ask your customers to refer you, new customers.

Tools and Resources

1. Hubspot CRM - https://www.hubspot.com/products/crm - A free CRM solution that interfaces beautifully with the other Hubspot products. Ideally suited for small businesses, it comes with all needed functionality and nothing that is unnecessary.

2. FreshSales - https://www.freshworks.com/freshsales-crm/ - A simple and easy-to-use CRM solution that has powerful capabilities to connect with your customers at all levels through multiple media and methods. Start with a free plan and scale up as you grow.

3. Insightly - https://www.insightly.com/ - Build ever stronger customer relationships with a one-page view of all customer-related data. Integrate with ease with more powerful applications as your business grows.

4. ConvergeHub - https://www.convergehub.com/ - A scalable solution that allows you to manage sales, marketing, customer connect, and billing all in one place. Stay in complete command of all your customer interactions at every touchpoint.

5. SugarCRM - https://www.sugarcrm.com/ - A solution ideally suited for small businesses, SugarCRM is highly customizable and developer-friendly. Add features as your needs expand. There is a very dedicated open-source group that continues to add to the software.

About the Author

Dr. Ali Asadi is an author, business coach, and international speaker. He specializes in helping professionals achieve success in today's highly competitive business environment. A well-respected entrepreneur who has written over ten books and e-books purchased by professionals and success seekers in many countries, Ali's wisdom on the many business topics is widely acclaimed.

Ali has more than twenty years of business management experience and focuses on all aspects of business management consulting and coaching. Ali is particularly knowledgeable and exceptionally skillful in analyzing your particular business needs and developing innovative techniques and proactive processes that can add value to your organization and increase profit potential. He takes a personal, hands-on approach, working directly with owners and senior executives to fine-tune business strategies for maximum benefit to you and your business. This one-on-one personal relationship with clients ranging from start-ups to well-established firms has served him well in many different fields, including medical services, transportation, construction, agriculture, technology, interior design, and retail. People truly appreciate his caring and sincere approach to helping them achieve success in their business ventures.

Dr. Asadi's Books:

Ali has written valuable books in diverse management subjects such as Marketing, Human Resource Management, Business Success Rules, and so on. The common denominator in all of these books is practical tips derived from his past work with clients in different industries. This is the reason for the popularity of his books. Ali's books can be ordered via top booksellers such as Amazon.com, Barnes and Noble, and Apple store.

Visit Dr. Asadi's Amazon page:
http://www.amazon.com/Ali-Asadi/e/B0082BCZR0

Book Dr. Asadi to Speak:

Ali's presentations draw from a large resource pool of training materials that are at a high tempo, effective and at the same time entertaining to his audience. Ali's competency lies in his innate ability to explain business solutions and needs in an understandable manner. Ali's talks can be customized for a particular audience. His ability to put forth a series of ideas and strategies is unique and facts, humor, insights are interweaved with practical concepts that the audience can relate to and apply promptly to get great results.

Business Consulting and Coaching with Dr. Asadi:

We are in a world where change is the only constant; businesses keep evolving and get more competitive. In such a scenario, it is difficult to keep up with the changes in the industry and the market place as wells as learning new business success tools and techniques. Therefore, getting a business coach isn't a luxury but a necessity that you must have in order to steer your business to safety and prosperity.

Ali gives you a true picture of your business and brings new ideas to improve it. Whether you are well established, or you are just starting off, you will always gain from the advice of a good business coach. Ali will show you different tools and techniques that will help your business succeed. If you are going to hire new employees, market your products or services, cut your business expenses, and so on, Dr. Asadi can help you understand the issues involved and help you make the right decisions. Business coaching/Consulting aids you in becoming more open and receptive to various innovative techniques of marketing your products and services. Business improvement techniques such as process classification, planning, automation, and improvement can be difficult to handle if your firm has never done them before.

Dr. Asadi's Business Coaching Procedures:

Ali's coaching/consulting procedure will help you identify your problems, get over your weaknesses, and find new ways to promote your products and services. Ali will also help you develop more and more innovative ideas for making people aware of your business and services.

Here is Ali's Coaching Procedure:

- Analyzing your current business processes and the overall impact towards achieving the organizational goals

- Helping you find gaps in areas where processes can be improved for greater efficiency and effectiveness

- Determining the underlying cause of any problem areas and work towards

- Identifying possible solutions to address the same

- Conducting a cost-benefit analysis to arrive at the best solution

- Providing step by step guidelines for implementation of the recommended solution

Clients include:

- Corporate Executives
- Business Owners
- Human Resource Managers
- Marketing Managers Service
- Professionals
- Whoever has the desire to improve his/her personal life and business

Visit his website at https://www.aasadi.com/ As you read his publications, you may have specific questions about how to apply the tips, tools, ideas, and strategies that the author discusses. Please email your questions to Dr. Ali Asadi at ali@aasadi.com. He will respond promptly and directly to you.

Connect with Dr. Ali Asadi through social media :

Facebook: https://www.facebook.com/aliasadipage/

Instagram: https://www.instagram.com/aliasadipage/

Twitter: https://twitter.com/ASADICONSULTING

LinkedIn: https://www.linkedin.com/in/aliasadi/

Index

Made in the USA
Monee, IL
15 January 2020